Our Lad Ricky

by
Michael Ruston

authorHOUSE®

AuthorHouse™ UK Ltd.
500 Avebury Boulevard
Central Milton Keynes, MK9 2BE
www.authorhouse.co.uk
Phone: 08001974150

First published by AuthorHouse 8/18/2008

ISBN: 978-1-4343-9863-5 (sc)

Printed in the United States of America
Bloomington, Indiana

This book is printed on acid-free paper.

Table of Contents

Chapter 1
SUCCESS AT LAST!

We had caught the No 74 bus from Stone Cross to Wolverhampton and had spent most of the half hour journey in silence. I was naturally nervous because it would be my third time at the recruiting office in Queen Street in the last six weeks. I had also made two other attempts to enlist, once in Birmingham and once in West Bromwich. The nearer we got to Wolverhampton the more nervous Ben was getting. Ben was going to sit my medical for me.

"You sure this will work Rick?" he asked.

"Course it will, the doc will just give you an eye 'n hearing test, listen to your chest and hey presto your in, or rather I'm in!" I replied.

"What if he starts asking awkward questions?" Ben moaned, "What will I tell him?"

"Trust me", I said, "He won't".

I did not tell Ben he would check his rear end, feel his balls and ask him to cough a couple of times. I thought I would leave that for him to find out for himself. If I had told him I was sure, he would chicken out.

"Tell you what!" I said, "I will give you five bob now, and the other five bob after, deal?" I fished a couple of half-crowns out of my pocket and handed them across. The original deal had been the ten bob if our little ruse was successful. Ten bob was a lot to me! Half a week's wages. We pulled into Queen Street, Wolverhampton. "Here we go Ben" I said getting up "Let's do the business".

The bus stop was in the middle of Queen Street and the Army Recruiting Office was down the end of the road, about a hundred yards from the stop. I could feel my stomach churning over and the closer we got the more nervous I got. Poor Ben looked petrified, "Piece of cake" I told him patting his back. "You'll walk it". When we got to the recruiting office, Ben continued to walk on past it as we previously planned. He would wait outside the Red Lion half way between the office and the doctors.

Taking a deep breath, I pushed open the door and walked in. The CSgt sitting at the desk looked up. "Hello lad" he said, then said "Oh it's not you again? I told you last time to leave it two or three months".

"I have been training" I said, "been doing morning and evening runs down the cut, I'm sure I'll pass this time".

The CSgt sighed loudly "Can't do it now son", he said, "you have to come back like I said, in two or three months"

At that Moment the door opened and a Major walked in "'morning CSgt, how's things this morning".

"Oh honky dory" he replied "was very quiet this week"

"And who is this young man?" he asked.

"Mr. Houghton" I told him.

"This is his third time here Sir", the CSgt told him "keeps failing his medical".

"Houghton, Houghton , that's familiar, have you been to Birmingham as well lad?"

"Yes Sir" I replied.

"And to West Bromwich?"

"Yes Sir".

"Thought so, you see lad, I am the OC for South Staffordshire, all those recruiting office's are part of the South Staffordshire Recruiting Team, never forget a name".

"Yes Sir" I said again. "You think you can pass this time lad?" asked the Major. "Oh Yes Sir! " I replied enthusiastically "I know I will".

"Ok, I will make a deal with you, if you fail; you don't come near any of my recruiting offices again until next year, if you pass all well and good!"

"Ok Sir - but I know I will pass".

The CSgt put together the forms necessary, sealed them in an envelope.

"Trust you know your way by now lad, off you go"

I took the envelope from the CSgt and headed for the door. Just as the door was closing behind me, I heard the CSgt tell the Major "He'll never pass so long as he's got a hole in his arse! - He suffers from asthma".

"Probably right" replied the Major.

Ben and I walked down the street to the Doctors' surgery.

"You're likely to drop us both in the shit!" moaned Ben.

I fished out the second installment of five bob and jiggled the coins under Bens nose.

"Easy money my mate, pass or fail the five bob is yours", I said, "You'll be in and out before you know it". We stopped twenty or so yards from the Doctors.

"There it is", I said pointing, "Come on mate, in you go" Ben took the envelope from me, "This better work" he said.

"It will" I replied sounding far more confident than I was actually feeling.

Following Ben's disappearance into the Surgery, I spent the next half of an hour pacing up and down nervously. It seemed to be taking an age. Finally, Ben appeared and before he got halfway towards me, he began shouting.

"You little bastard, you lying toe rag - you never said I had to drop my keks"

"Oh didn't I", I replied, "Must have slipped my mind."

"You're a conniving sneaky bastard Rick," exclaimed Ben "That bastard doctor spent ages just feeling my balls"

"Don't exaggerate Ben," I said, and then "Did you pass?"

"How the hell should I know, he never said".

I took the sealed envelope from Ben and when we arrived back at the Recruiting Office Ben carried on past to wait near the Bus Stop. When I walked back into the Recruiting Office the CSgt was not at his desk, but the Major was. "How'd you get on lad?" He asked holding out his hand to take the envelope from me.

"I think I passed" I replied the fear in my voice plain to hear.

"'Have a seat" said the Major running his finger under the flap of the envelope.

I sat down, my knees were beginning to tremble nervously and I was gripping my hands tightly together.

"Hmmm" remarked the Major as he reached up to scratch his forehead.

He looked at me and then back at the paperwork.

"Hmmmm!" He flicked over the page "Hu hu!"

He placed the paperwork in front of him and leaned on the desk.

"Raining out is it lad?" asked the Major.

"No Sir."

"Are you sure?"

"Yes Sir."

"Only it seems you have shrunk a bit since leaving the Doctors!" He remarked.

At that point, the CSgt returned with two large mugs of tea and some sandwiches. He placed a cup and a sandwich next to the Major. He took a sip of his tea.

"On here, lad, it says you are five feet eleven and weighing nine and a half stone, I would like to bet your not even five foot six and close to a seven stone weakling"

"Oh" I replied feeling my face getting hot. I went even redder as the Major leaned further across the desk gazing at me intently.

"Hmm, your eyes have gone a funny colour too" he said.

By this time, I was literally squirming in my seat and my face must have been blood red.

"Says here" the Major went on "You have brown eyes, your eyes are blue"

I started to jabber unintelligibly as I tried to get out of the predicament I now found myself in.

"Any of your family in the services?" he asked changing tack.

"My father was in the Royal Engineers," I stammered "And my brother is still in, been in six or seven years".

"You want to follow in their footsteps is that it?" enquired the Major.

"Yes Sir, I know I can do it", I replied, realising there was a glimmer of hope in this line of questioning. Suddenly the Major stood up, picked up his tea and sandwich. Turning to the CSgt, he said, "I'm not in! Moreover, let us not have this chappie in here again eh! Shall we?"

"Right oh!" replied the CSgt and took the Majors place at the desk.

He said nothing for a while just sat and looked at me. I tried hard to look him straight in the eye but found myself weakening by the second. He slammed his hand on the desk suddenly startling me; I almost jumped out of my skin.

"Let me make this clear lad, I'll give you three weeks, do you hear, three weeks, and when it all goes tits up, don't ever come crawling back here again, understood!"

"Yes CSgt" I said, excitement building up inside me, was I in? The CSgt pulled a variety of forms from the drawers making a neat pile in front of him. He began to write. Completing the first two forms, he passed them across to me.

"Official Secrets Act, sign there", I signed.

He wrote some more.

"Attestation Papers, signing on for the minimum of six years, sign there". I signed. He took a little New Testament Bible, wrote my name in and handed it over. He gave me a brand new shilling piece.

"The Queens Shilling" he informed me, "treasure it, it will be a souvenir of your brief sojourn as a serving soldier, I still have mine".

Removing a cash tin from the drawer, he took out and filled in a Bus Warrant from Stone Cross to Birmingham Snow Hill and a Train Warrant from Birmingham Snow Hill to Cove, Farnborough, both single. "You have to report to No 1 Training Regiment, Royal Engineers, Cove near Farnborough, Hants by 9 0' clock next Monday, So you will probably have to travel down on Sunday, understood."

"Yes CSgt".

From the cash box, the CSgt removed a one-pound note, a ten-shilling note and some small change.

"You will be on unpaid leave until next Monday" he said "This is your first weeks pay starting Monday, look after it you will need it", he said

"Yes CSgt"

The CSgt gathered up all the papers and stuffed them into an A4 envelope. I picked up my first weeks pay. Standing up he thrust out his hand.

"I wish you luck my lad, you're going to need it!" he said "But I'm not holding my breath".

"I'll be OK CSgt," I said and taking the envelope I turned and almost ran from the Recruiting Office fearful he would change his mind.

Out in the street I began jumping up and down "Yahoooo!" I screamed, "I'm in!"

Several people in the street stopped and stared, who cares, I thought, I ran to Ben and threw my arms around him trying unsuccessfully to lift him up. "I did it, I did it, I'm in" I shouted, laughing uncontrollably at the same time.

"You mean I bloody did it!" shouted Ben.

"Yeah we did it, we did it".

We both began to run down the street towards the Bus Stop laughing and jumping up and down as we ran. I could not resist a look back towards the Recruiting Office as we ran and I saw the Major standing outside the door. I waved the envelope at him and shaking his head he turned and went back inside.

All the way back to Stone Cross on the bus I talked continually about all the places I was going to see, the things I was going to do. Ben hardly said a word but I could see he was pleased for me as he had a half smile on his face the whole time, patiently listening to my incoherent ramblings. I had tried to convince Ben to enlist too. He would not even try. Ben was a bed-wetter, I was not sure if he knew I knew, we never talked about it, but I knew that was the reason he would not try to join up. As we got back to Stone Cross, I swore Ben to secrecy, "If my Mom gets wind of this before the weekend", I said "she'll move heaven and earth to stop me from going". The Parental Consent form I had handed included a rather vague imitation of my fathers signature on it. From Stone Cross, Ben and I began the fifteen-minute walk home. He was still strangely silent. "What's up?" I asked him "Aren't you happy?"

"Its OK for you" he replied "You will probably make a load of new mates, a few weeks down the line you will have forgotten your old school mate Ben."

"Don't be daft" I said, horrified at the thought, "You'll still be my best mate, and nothing will ever change that. We'll have a good get together when I come home on leave".

His fears put a dampener on my erstwhile enthusiasm and we walked the remainder of the way home without a word. The funny thing is Ben had been right, when I thanked him again at his house for the hundredth time since leaving Wolverhampton and he went inside and closed the door, it was the last time I saw Ben from that day to this!

What a week I had! Having walked home with Ben I arrived home determined to keep quiet until Friday or Saturday to try to make sure my Mom did not find out about my enlistment. However no sooner had I walked in the door I bumped into one of my elder brothers, Don.

"What you looking so pleased about?" he asked.

"Nothing, why?" I had replied.

"You look like you just won the pools," he said. My brothers could read me like a book.

I thought I could trust Don with my secret.

"Promise not to say anything?" I told him.

"Slit me throat 'ope to die," he said running a finger beneath his chin.

"I joined up today, the Royal Engineers, like Dad and Jamie".

"You're bloody joking!" exclaimed Don "the army would kill you!"

"Didn't do Dad or Jamie any harm" I retorted.

"You won't last five minutes, besides Mom would never let you go!"

"I'm not telling Mom till Saturday, it will be too late then". Before long my two other brothers, Paul and Kev and my sister Charlotte were in on it and it became a foregone conclusion that Mom would find out before the day was out.

I managed to hold out until my Dad got home, as I felt sure he would be my one true ally. There followed several hours of argument and counter-argument lasting late into the evening with my siblings throwing constant scorn and contempt at the mere thought of my joining the army. My parents argued long and hard. My Dad put forward the argument that if my Mom, brothers and sister thought I would not last more than a week or two the best thing all round was to let me go and at least get the whole idea out of my system. After all, next year I would be eighteen and they would not be able to stop me anyway. Having put this argument forward several times and no one being able to produce an alternative and convincing reason why I should not go, it became accepted that I would. Don ended all argument by saying "It'll be a good excuse of a piss-up Sunday Dinner time at any rate".

My mother spent all her energies on Wednesday, Thursday and Friday trying to convince me of the foolishness of my enlisting. Nevertheless, I was resolute. On Saturday she got out a paper carrier bag in which she placed a spare shirt, a grey looking hand towel in which was rolled a used bar of soap, my Dads old shaving brush and cut throat razor.

"I'll do you some sandwiches and a bottle of tea on Sunday morning to take with you," she said. There were no luxury items such as a toothbrush or underwear.

I am not sure any of us had any!

Chapter 2
JOURNEY SOUTH

The next few days dragged by. I was constantly mocked by my siblings and moaned at by my mother who desperately tried to get me to change my mind. However, Sunday arrived at long last and my family and I were making our way to Stone Cross, which opened at twelve noon, for my farewell piss up. I wore a Grey flannel shirt, a slightly too big bright green v necked pullover which had belonged to Don, a pair of brown corduroy trousers and a pair of brown lace up boots. Over all of this, I wore a black, slightly too small duffle coat, which was a very tight fit if I buttoned it up. The sleeves ending halfway between wrist and elbow. However, it was a warm duffle coat! Mom had pulled up a bit of lino from the pantry and cut two insoles for my boots in a bid to keep the water out should it rain.

Mom was carrying my paper carrier bag containing my spare shirt and things and also a couple of rounds of beef dripping, a couple of rounds of lemon curd and a milk bottle of tea with a screwed up piece of bread paper stuffed in the top to act as a stopper. The pub was called the Golden Lion but everyone called it the Cross! I had been there many times but never of course actually inside the bar or lounge. Kids were strictly off limits and the landlord, Harry, would never allow anyone under eighteen to have so much as a sniff of beer, not in *his* public house. I was almost seventeen and half and wondered how I was going to get a sniff of beer with Harry around.

When we arrived at the Cross, we walked around the back to the lounge where it would be less busy. My Dad opened the lounge door and waved me on in. He and I walked up to the bar together while my Mom and brothers took up seats close by. Harry was standing at the bar polishing a tray of glasses.

"All right Jamie" he said greeting my Dad.

"Alright Harry," replied my Dad "That'll be four and a half pints of M&B, two bottles of pop and two packets of crisps, please Harry".

Harry did not move a Park Drive dangling from the corner of his mouth.

"You know Rick" Dad said "Joined the Army he has and he's off this afternoon to report in".

"Didn't know you was eighteen my boy" said Harry looking me in the face.

"He's old enough to serve Queen and Country" Dad replied for me "And he'd like to buy his old man a pint before he shoots off".

Harry held the glass he was polishing up to the light, breathed on it before giving it another wipe. "Sounds fair to me" said Harry and began pouring the first pint into the glass he had just polished. Dad gave me a nudge and held his hand out below the counter and out of sight of my family and Harry. He held three crisp One Pound notes.

"You can get the first round son" he said "And the change will keep you going till you get yourself straight". "I don't need that Dad," I said, "I got thirty bob or more". "Take it son," he said, "Don't go insulting' your old man in front of other people." I took the three pounds and handed one of them over to Harry to pay for the round.

I had drunk beer a few times, such as on my birthday and at Christmas, but never a whole pint all at once. I passed Mom her half and a pint each to my brothers while Dad took the pop and crisps to Charlotte and Paul out in the corridor. The plan had been for me to have one or two pints and catch the half past one bus to Birmingham. I had barely had my third sip of my pint when Kev banged his empty glass on the table. "Ahhh! That was just what the doctor ordered," he exclaimed "Your round is it now Dad?" To my horror, Dad plonked another pint in front of my brothers, and me then leaning down whispered loud enough for my brothers to hear. "Take your time son; you don't want to end up getting pissed before you even get started". I tried hard to take his advice but in due course a third and a fourth pint came and went.

During the next couple of hours, I did not have a watch and had forgotten to keep an eye on the time. "One for the road then ah kid" Don said, "You've missed the half one bus." "Oh no!" I groaned, "next one's not till 'half two". Don was already on his way to the bar and a fifth and I hoped a final pint was plonked down on the table before me. As it happened, I developed hiccups shortly after and to the great amusement of the family spent the next half hour or so trying to get rid of them. Apart from a couple of trips to the toilet, I had not moved much since getting there. Now, on my third trip, I was really feeling the effects of the four and a bit pints staggering to the left and then the right as I made my way out. Inside the toilet, the hiccups had not abated and I began to feel decidedly ill.

I could feel beer sloshing and lapping around at the base of my throat. "I'm going to throw up" I said to myself aloud and made a dash for the cubicle slamming the door open as I went in. I barely made it, as I approached the toilet the four pints came gushing out. I spent a good five minutes retching and feeling very sorry for myself. Taking a wad of toilet paper, I wiped my mouth and streaming eyes before returning even more unsteadily to the lounge.

As soon as I walked in my brothers laughed and received a withering look that should have killed them on the spot from my Mom.

"You OK son?" asked Dad.

"I'm fine," I slurred thankful that the hiccups had miraculously disappeared.

"OK, well if you still want to catch the 'half two bus we better make a move".

So saying the family all picked up their beers and drained what was left. I looked down at my last pint, which was still more than half full.

"I'd leave it if I were you son," said Dad patting me on the shoulder "You'll have plenty more to come".

Mom took my arm and we traipsed outside and crossed the road to the bus stop. Mom was doing her best to keep me moving in a straight line. I could see she was upset and then suddenly, to my surprise, realized that they were all upset. Even my brother's eyes were moistening up a little. Within ten minutes, the bus arrived.

"You don't have to son", Dad said, "No one will think the worse of you if you changed your mind".

I felt my resolve weakening, Mom stood there blowing her nose and my family all standing around looking miserable.

Nevertheless, I knew that if I did not go it would be to please the family, not myself, and that ultimately I would regret it.

"No Dad", I said a sob rising in my throat "I've come this far and I have to go" Mom sobbed loudly and nearly broke my neck with a huge hug and then not wanting to let go". Dad came to my rescue and eased her arms from around my neck. We shook hands. I think that was the first time I had ever shook hands with my Dad and I could feel the tears welling up. I coughed loudly and turning to my brothers. "C'ya Kev, Don, behave yourselves".

I shook hands with them too and then giving Charlotte and Paul a quick hug, I boarded the bus. As I did so, the conductor rang the bell and the bus pulled away. The family stood there waving until the bus disappeared around the corner.

I went upstairs on the bus and sat at the front. No sooner had I sat down I realized I needed another pee. I spent the next half hour in excruciating discomfort wriggling and banging my knees together in order to stave off a disaster. I barely managed to hold out until I got to West Bromwich where the bus halted for about ten minutes. Having received the permission of the conductor I made another mad dash for the toilet. By the time I got to Birmingham, some forty-five minutes later I had the beginnings of a huge hangover that would trouble me for most of my journey south and I was again in need of relief.

However, the bus stop in Birmingham was a good fifteen minutes walk from Snow Hill Station and not being able to find a toilet took relief alongside a huge willow tree in the grounds of a large church, which just happened to be along the route. It was about five o'clock when I finally got to Snow Hill. I handed in my train warrant in exchange for a ticket and enquired about train timings. "Just missed the four fifty" the teller told me "Next train is at six forty five, gets into London eight twenty eight" What the ticket office didn't tell me, was that train was a mail train, and stopped at practically every station between Birmingham and London and that the train I had just missed would have got to London in half the time.

I found the platform and feeling ever so slightly better opened up my carrier bag and pulled out a large packet wrapped in greaseproof bread paper. Opening it up on my lap I took out a couple of thick slices of bread between which was smothered a thick layer of beef dripping, my favourite. Having munched my beef dripping sandwiches I re-wrapped the remainder for later and taking out my bottle of tea, which was cold by this time, I took a hearty swig.

I spent the next hour pacing up and down impatiently, waiting for the train, my fathers words "You don't have to go" running round and round my head. But I knew I did have to go. Finally, the train did arrive and I climbed aboard. The carriage did not appear to have heating and it was getting decidedly chilly. I pulled the duffle coat closer around me, pulled the hood up, and settled down.

Eventually the train chugged out of Snow Hill gently picking up speed and soon the lights of Snow Hill and Birmingham disappeared behind me. No sooner had the old train reached its maximum speed it appeared to me that the driver took his foot from the accelerator and we began to slow down again.

Within twenty minutes of departure, we were pulling into what would seem to me the first of hundreds of little stations between Birmingham and London. The only highlight being the occasional fellow passengers that came into my carriage and who all appeared to be local commuters on their way home. The only one I spoke to was a young lady in her late teens with a large beehive hairdo, tight fitting blouse in danger of spilling its contents and a mini skirt I had previously only dreamed about. Oh and white knickers! She had said "Hello" as she entered the carriage and sat opposite me. I could not face her directly as I had difficulty in knowing where to look. What she did not know was that she had a perfectly good reflection in the carriage window, which I made full use of. Unfortunately, she was only with me for two or three stops and hopped off at Coventry. I remember thinking if they are all like that in Coventry I ought to pay it a visit sometime.

The minutes stretching agonizingly slowly into hours and each time we slowed to a halt I would raise from my slumber, cock open one eye and check my progress towards London. Eventually we arrived at Watford Junction and I knew then that I was within half an hour of the capital city. It was just before eight according to the clock hanging above the platform. I pulled the paper carrier bag from its position between myself and the carriage wall and fished out the second of my beef dripping sandwiches. I ate that and then the lemon curd sandwiches after which I finished off the cold tea, disposing of the bottle on the luggage rack above my head. The greaseproof paper from my beef dripping and lemon curd sandwiches I stuffed down the back of my seat. I liked to leave the place nice and tidy when I left.

The train finally pulled into London Euston shortly after half past eight and I made my way towards the famed underground system. I had to go to London Victoria to continue on to Cove. The journey time I was told was only about twenty minutes from Euston to Victoria. Well it would have been had I got on the right underground train to start with. What had confused me were the signs saying Bakerloo or Victoria or Central Line North and Bakerloo or Victoria or Central Line South. I had guessed I would need a southbound route! I do not know. All I do know was the journey took practically an hour and I had to change trains three times before finally getting to Victoria Station.

By the time, I walked into Victoria Station it was getting close to ten o'clock. Again I was informed that I had "just missed" my train and had to wait almost an hour for the next which, you guessed it, was another mail train. My train journey from London to Cove was uneventful and I cat napped most of the way arriving at about one o'clock in the morning. Getting off my train at Cove, it was pitch dark with not a soul about. I did detect a faint light inside the ticket office, which had the blind drawn down. Beside the ticket office was a blackboard, which informed me that the last transport to 1 & 3 Training Regiments departs at 11 p.m. The first would be at approximately 7.30 a.m.

I could see someone moving about in the ticket office and so knocked on the window.

"Closed!" was the shouted response.

"Have you got a minute?" I called back.

I heard him swear under his breath and a chair slide noisily backward. Then the blind moved upwards to reveal an elderly gent with a steaming hot mug of tea and a massive cheese toasted sandwich. My stomach churned over at the sight of the tea and toast.

"I've missed the transport to Cove. How far is it?" I asked him. I did not like the idea of spending the next six hours or more sitting in a cold draughty waiting room.

"Not far", he replied "take less than hour probably - go out the station, down to your left, turn right at he traffic lights and just keep going, no turns, you'll get to the barracks on the right hand side". I thanked him and tucking my carrier bag under my arm made my way out of the station following the route indicated by the ticket man.

Cove was a small country village with not much more than a pub, post office and corner shop. I had not been walking for more than ten minutes when I realized that I would be leaving the streetlights behind, the lane snaking off into the darkness. I did think about going back to the train station but what the hell, I am a rough and tough soldier now convincing myself there was nothing to be afraid of. Another ten minutes down the country lane I found that I was singing, "old MacDonald had a farm" to myself rather nervously. A distant rumble of thunder encouraged me to sing a little louder and walk a little faster.

It was not long before I felt the first drops of rain on my face and down the back of my neck. I pulled the hood of the duffle coat up over my head but as the coat was two sizes too small, the hood would not stay up, unless I held it up, so I let it go. A flash of lightening behind me made me jump. I began to sing to myself even louder and walked even faster. Then the heavens opened and it began to pour. It was the worst downpour I had experienced for a long time and within no time; I was soaked to the skin. The lino in my boots had not helped that much but they made a comforting squelching noise as I walked. Then, there, yes! I could see lights.

I came to a large barbed wire fence with a sign, which said 'WD Property Keep Out'. About a hundred yards further on I saw a floodlit area and the gate. When I got to the gate, a man not much older than me emerged from a sentry box.

"Just arrived," I told him needlessly. He nodded towards a long low building off to one side "Guardroom" he said indicating that is where I should report to with a jerk of his thumb.

Moving around the barrier, I mounted the steps to the Guardroom and knocked on the door. A man was sitting at the window reading. He looked up and then, ignoring my presence, continued with his paper or book.

I waited for a minute or two then knocked again, a little louder. The man looked up, slid the window open.

"You knock that bloody door again and I'll rip you bloody arm off".

I stepped back aghast. He had sworn at me. I never swore! I could not believe what I had heard and could feel my indignation and anger rising. How dare he talk to me like that!

The young man emerged once more from his guard hut by the gate. He pointed at the door. I made a knocking sign while shaking my head and pointing at the man in the window. The man made as if reading a book, drew a square and pointed at the door. I turned and looked again at the door I had been knocking and noticed for the first time a small white piece of paper attached to the door with a couple of drawing pins. I walked back up the steps to the door and in the dim light read:

"ALL ENQUIRIES AT THE WINDOW"

Below the sign was an arrow pointing to the man in the window. Nervously I went up to the window and was just about to knock on it when the man, without looking up from his paper, pointed down to where there was a little white button with the word "PRESS" on it. I pressed. The man looked up smiling sweetly and slowly opened the window.

"Good Morning, Sir, can I help you." He said helpfully.

"I have just arrived," I said

"Never" replied the man in the window "Have you really?"

Then stepping back he shouted "Smith! Get your miserable little arse out here now!"

There was a sound of running feet and a sleepy eyed lad appeared by the man at the window standing smartly to attention.

"Take this, 'er gentleman, to the transit accommodation and make sure he is made comfortable" turning to me he said "I am the Provost Sgt, I am sure I will resume our acquaintance in due course" and with that he slammed the window shut.

The young man came out of the guardroom having put on a rain shield and led me off down the road. Very shortly, we arrived at a building he referred to as a 'Spider' due to the fact that three large rooms protruded from each side. He walked in and turned on the light in the first room he came to.

There were two big wood stoves in the room with buckets of wood and coke.

"If you want to light the fire you can, but if you do you have to clean it out and relay it before breakfast," he told me.

"Take your pick," he said with a sweep of his arm.

There were ten beds evenly spaced out on each side of the room. On each bed, there was a straw mattress, one pillow and three blankets.

"No sheets?" I asked the lad

"Tomorrow" he replied and left.

I rolled out the mattress and placed a blanket over it. Removing my boots, I lay down on the bed and pulled the remaining two blankets up and over my body.

It was very cold as I lay in bed, feeling very wet and damp, blankets over my head, shivering.

"Don't think I will sleep like this," I thought to myself but with a feeling of some elation whispered to myself "but I'm here. I've arrived".

Chapter 3
D-DAY

I was suddenly woken by a horrendous din, as a dustbin was thrown the entire length of the room and dazzled as all the lights in the room were switched on.

"Come on you lot" someone was shouting at the top of his voice.

"Hands off your cocks and on with your socks, up! Up! Up! Lets be having you".

I rolled off the bed rubbing my eyes and very conscious of the warm dampness of my clothes. I was amazed to find that there were four others in the room who had arrived after me and I had not heard a thing!

"My name is Cpl Harper, not Harpic before anyone has any bright ideas, Harper. I am your Training NCO, for the next nineteen weeks, I am God - got that".

There was a murmur of "Yes, Cpl".

"I said have you got that?" He shouted. "I cannot hear you!"

"Yes, Cpl!" we screamed.

The Cpl did a circuit of the room and finished up standing in front of me.

"I must make sure I am not the first in line next time" I thought to myself "be less conspicuous".

The Cpl stood looking me up and down.

"Name?" he asked, "Houghton" I said. He ran his finger down his clipboard and presumably having found my name made a tick against it.

"Oh dear! Oh dear!" he exclaimed rocking back on forth on his heels.

"What have we got here?" He put his stick to my back and eased me forward a pace before walking around me.

"tut tut tut! He said.

Then poking his stick into a hole in the centre of my bright green v-neck pullover he asked, "You not heard of a needle and cotton where you come from?"

I thought better of answering.

"Well lad, have you?" he shouted

"Yes, Cpl" I replied.

"Louder" he shouted

"Yes Cpl" I shouted back.

Moving a little to my left, he pushed his stick into another hole at my right elbow.

"Well don't they know how to use a needle and cotton then where you come from lad?"

"Yes, Cpl" I shouted again.

"Well lad" he said, "before I see this, this, this excuse for a pullover again, I suggest you find a needle and cotton and use them."

"Yes, Cpl" I shouted.

"And on this too" he said tapping the nail of my big toe which was sticking out from a hole in my sock. With that, he moves on to the next lad.

"Name?" Asked the Cpl.

"Duncan-Forbes, Cpl" came the immediate response. He had a very posh accent like, as my father would say, he had marbles in his mouth. He was wearing a very posh pair of pyjamas and a dressing gown to match.

"I am not in the habit of being on first name terms with dummies like you," the Cpl shouted.

"No Cpl, my name is Peter Duncan-Forbes."

"Oh! I see that one surname is not good enough for you eh?" Asked the Cpl.

"Duncan-Forbes is the family name Cpl, passed from father to son" explained the man.

"Don't get smart with me lad" shouted the Cpl. Then after a moment's hesitation asked "And who might your father be lad?"

"Lt-Colonel Duncan-Forbes, Worcestershire & Sherwood Foresters!" replied the man "Father thought I should go through normal basic training in the Royal Engineers before going to Sandhurst," he went on "stand me in good stead he said"

"Did he now" said the Cpl looking disgusted "We will have to see won't we".

The Cpl moved on to the other two new arrivals, a Scotsman and a Londoner giving them similar treatment and verbal harassment until he finished up back at the door leading into the room.

"Right you 'orrible lot, breakfast is from six until seven. You have ten minutes to shit, shower and shave and get over to the cookhouse for breakfast. I will be back at seven o'clock" with that he did a smart about

25

turn and marched out the room slamming the door behind him. I dug out my brown paper carrier bag from under the bed and took out my grubby looking hand towel, not much bigger than your average tea towel and headed for the ablutions. I did not bother with a shower, just washing hands and face. I had my father's old shaving brush and cutthroat razor between the taps. The posh lad, Peter, was at the next sink.

"My goodness!" he exclaimed, "I've never seen a razor like that before, where did you get it from?"

"It was my Dads," I informed him.

"Amazing" he said "can I?"

"Help yourself," I told him and he picked it up and opened it. It was a bit grubby but that just seemed to impress him all the more.

"This is great," he said having a practice swing around his cheeks. I looked at his posh bag. His razor was the latest; you twisted the handle to open the top, a brilliant shaving brush the handle of which looked as if it was made from ivory. He even had a little flannel and a matching container for his soap. Not only did he have toothbrush and toothpaste he had a little ceramic cup to gargle with. His towel looked brand new and it was huge, I could have wrapped it around me two or three times.

"Oh how the other half live" I thought to myself.

Back in the room Jock and Tam, the Londoner, were ready to go to the cookhouse and the four of us left together. We had not gone more than twenty yards when a Sgt with a red sash came and bawled us out for not marching in file and in step. When we got to the cookhouse, we found that everyone had their own mess tins, mug, knife, fork and spoon. It was left to

Peter to tackle the Chefs to borrow a plate, a pint pot for us to share a cup of tea in and a fork each. When the Chefs plonked a rasher of bacon, one sausage, one egg, a tablespoon of beans, a tomato and half a slice of fried bread onto my plate I thought I had died and gone to heaven! It was the best breakfast I had ever tasted, superb, the plate swimming in lovely grease!

Peter gave me his fried bread picking it up between forefinger and thumb and dropping it on my plate with a look of sheer disgust on his face.

"This is disgusting" Peter complained.

"Aye, I've had better" confirmed Jock and Tam just picked at it with his fork looking decidedly unsure. By the end of breakfast, I had profited by another two sausages, a hard fried egg and a rasher of bacon. Yummy!

When we got back to our room, every bed was taken. Apparently, two truckloads of recruits had been collected from the station and, we heard, there were more on the way. Peter made the mistake of sitting on my bed talking with me when the Cpl returned bang on seven o'clock.

"What on earth do you think you are all doing?" He screamed.

We had all been sitting awaiting his return.

"Well?" He shouted.

"Nothing, Cpl" several voices ventured hesitantly.

"Nothing?" he shouted back at them "Nothing, I will give you nothing?"

He marched over to a metal cupboard in the corner of the room. I had not noticed the cupboard before. He flung open its doors grabbed the first thing that came to hand which just happened to be a bottle of windowlene.

"You" he said throwing the windowlene and a duster in the direction of Peter and I.

I caught them.

"Clean the windows" He threw a duster at Peter, "Windowsills, lockers and skirting boards".

Within two minutes of him entering the room everyone was busy dusting, sweeping, mopping, polishing and cleaning like there was no tomorrow. We continued our cleaning chores for a good hour or more not daring to be caught not doing anything incase he reappeared as if by magic.

He did return as if by magic because in he sweeps running fingers over furniture, doors and windowsills checking for any microscopic specks of dirt or dust.

He approached to inspect my windows.

"Those are diabolical" he shouted, "what's wrong with those?" Waving his stick at the upper windows.

"I cannot reach" I explained, "I'm not tall enough".

"I can't reach, I'm not tall enough", he mimicked in a childlike voice. He walked over to a chair and putting his foot on the seat pushed it across the room towards me.

"Use your initiative lad, think! There is no such thing as I can't".

And so with one foot precariously balanced on the back of the chair and the other on the window ledge, I hitched myself upwards so I could reach the top windows. But only just. The Cpl lost interest in me and busied himself with making Peter, Tam and Jock miserable for a while before walking back towards me.

"Good Morning, Cpl" I heard a new voice, even posher than Peters, remark.

"Is everything alright?"

"All under control Sir "replied the Cpl coming smartly to attention and saluting.

"Jolly Good! Jolly Good!" Came the voice.

I tried to look over my shoulder at the new comer.

Then. disaster struck. One minute I was perched on the chair-cum-windowsill, next second I was flat on my back and the chair skidding across the floor. All the wind had been knocked out of my body when I hit the floor, there were stars before my eyes, and I could not speak!

When I did recover sufficiently to realize what was happening around me the newcomer, a Lt, was leaning over me and screaming blue murder at me.

"You silly imbecile, what do you think you were doing standing on the back of the chair, have you no common sense? Are you totally insane?"

My vision cleared sufficient to see a Lt standing over me in his best No. 2 Dress uniform complete with Sam Browne, Sword and Medal Ribbon. From his left shoulder, down diagonally across his chest, to his waist were several streaks of fresh windowlene. It was now dripping from his tunic onto the sharp creases in his trousers.

"Look what you have done!" He shouted taking another step towards me.

To my utter horror, I noticed that the windowlene bottle was still perched dangerously on top of his peaked cap gently oozing its contents down the side. He must have then felt it drip onto his ear and his cheek.

"What the!" he cried snatching his cap from his head.

The windowlene bottle dropped down between his feet smashing into a thousand pieces and spraying his highly polished brown shoes with the bright pink cleaner.

"Aaargh! " He screamed. I could see his face going purple and the veins on his neck bulging outward.

"You! You! You!" He shouted pointing and shaking his peak cap at me. Then, completely lost for words he suddenly turned and stomped out brushing at his hat and tunic.

The Cpl came over and helped me up. He stood looking at me for a moment realizing I could have said that it was he who had made me use the chair.

"You OK lad?" He asked

"I'm fine" I replied.

"Well" said the Cpl "You certainly know how to impress! Get this mess cleaned up" and he walked away, half a smile on his face. A short while later a Sgt arrived and introduced himself as Sgt Steel.

"I would like to meet the young man who has so impressed the Party Officer Lt Mortimer" he asked gazing around the room. Looking from man to man.

"Well?" He demanded.

"You must mean me Sgt," I shouted out stepping forward.

He came forward and stood in front of me, staring me in the eye for a long minute.

"Just wanted to remember your name and face," he said in a low voice.

It was now gone ten in the morning. "Right!" he shouted, "Outside on the road, three ranks move!" When we all ran out, we found that all the other rooms were already outside and in their ranks. There were seventy-nine of us. The Party Officer appeared wearing denim and a heavy duty pullover. He looked up and down the ranks for several minutes before speaking.

"I am Lt Mortimer your Party Officer; you are all members of 125 Training Party. You will have met Sgt Steel and your respective Room Training NCOs. You are going to be trained as Royal Engineers and become members of one of the oldest and finest Corps in the British Army" he paused for breath and then said "If there is anyone here who feels that this is not for him then fall out now and report to the troop office".

He passed his gaze over the ranks. I had the uncomfortable feeling that he was looking for me! To my surprise, someone did actually fall out and go back inside. But not from my room.

"Alright Sgt carry On" With that our Party Officer did a smart about turn and disappeared back inside the Spider. He was probably disappointed that he had not been able to wear his nice service dress uniform.

Our room Training NCOs took over and half of us were marched away to the bedding store and the other half to the clothing and equipment store. I was with the bedding store lot. We were told we would not be returning to the transit Spider but to Spider number 10, which was twice as far across the other side of the parade ground. Inside the bedding store, we were given a mattress cover in which was thrown two pillows, two pillow cases, two sheets, one blanket U.S., three serviceable blankets and a bed cover. They weighed a ton. Hitching the mattress cover and its contents over my shoulder, I made my way out towards Spider No 10.

I saw a staggered line of young men all carrying their bedding and making their way across the parade ground towards Spider 10 and followed them. We were almost halfway across when the Sgt with the Red Sash reappeared giving us all hell.

"What the hell do you think your doing on my Parade Ground?" he screamed at us. "No-one but no-one walks across my parade ground - off! off!"

He pointed his stick the way we had come. One or two enterprising lads tried to veer off to the left as a short cut.

"No! Off!" he shouted, "the way you came".

So we all had to retrace our steps and commence a three times as long trek around the parade ground. By this time, I had to make regular stops on the way to rest. To make matters worse it was starting to rain again.

Luckily, for Peter he had seen what was happening and had not tried to cross the parade ground. He was way ahead of us by this time. I was half way round the parade ground when Peter came trotting back.

"Need a hand?" He asked. I was far too puffed out to answer and my bedding was getting wetter by the minute. He took the mattress cover from me and slung it over his shoulder with ease. Our beds already had foam mattresses when we arrived at Spider 10 and having dumped our bedding on to our beds we were immediately paraded and marched away to the clothing store. If I thought that had been hard going, boy the next load was twice as hard.

Inside the clothing, store the civilian store men did not ask our sizes but began to dish out clothing and equipment at super speed. "Kit Bag, open it! Open it" they shouted. Then "from the top, tin helmet, one, helmet liner, one, cam net, one, beret blue, one, vests, two, PT vest white, one, PT vest red, one, PT shorts, blue, two, shirts hairy, two, pullover lightweight, one, pullover heavy duty, one, battledress tunic, one, jackets denim, two". And so they went on all the way down to "Boots Hobnail, one, boots DMS, one!"

We had to continually shake our kitbags to get the mass of our new clothing in and the further we went down the line the heavier it got. I could scarcely lift it never mind shake it by the time I was half way down the line.

Having crammed so much clothing into my kitbag, I could hardly lift the damn thing. I then I had to cross to the other side of the storeroom whereupon a large pack was thrust into my arms!

"Open it, Open it!" the store man screamed at me.

Once open, in went ammunition pouch left, ammunition pouch right, water bottle, water bottle holder, bayonet frog, mess tin small, mess tin large, knife, fork, spoon, pint mug, small pack, weapon cleaning kit, belts, kicking straps, shoulder straps . . . and on and on it went. I was dragging my kit bag along the floor as my large pack was getting stuffed full of all sorts of webbing and equipment over the other. Eventually I staggered back to the door I had come in Kit bag over one shoulder, large pack over the other and my knees beginning to buckle under the sheer weight of it all.

My room Training NCO was waiting outside.

"Can I leave my kit bag here" I asked "and take this lot first?" indicating my large pack.

"No you bloody well can't" he shouted. He helped me on with the large pack so that I was wearing it properly on my back and with a swift swoop of the arms lifted my kit bag and plonked it on top. He took each of my hands and placed them either side of my kit bag behind my neck and give me a gentle shove forward.

I was almost bent double with the weight. I tried to take a few steps but immediately fell to my knees and then flat on my face.

"Oh for goodness sake" moaned the Cpl "come on!"

He lifted the kit bag up and he carried it for me around the parade ground to Spider No 10.

The next few hours were taken up with showing us how our equipment went together. How it was to be ironed and stored in our lockers. How to make our bed packs. (A blanket, then a sheet and blanket, then the second sheet and another blanket, all squared off nice and neatly wrapped with our bed cover). We were even told how to use toilet paper!

"Three sheets per man per visit"; we were told "one up, one down, one to polish!"

We were then shown how we were to lay out our equipment on the bed for inspection each morning. Having laid mine out the Cpl spotted my cutthroat razor. "What the hell do you call this?" he asked "this is an offensive weapon."

"Its my Dads razor" I replied.

"You are not going to actually shave with this?" He asked

"Yes, Cpl".

"You are likely to do yourself a mischief" he said, "Haven't you got a proper razor?"

"No Cpl".

"Well I suggest you go and buy one," he said, "because that thing is confiscated". With that, he took my Dads cutthroat razor and slipped it into his pocket. I never saw it again.

A 'school' type timetable for 'This Week' and 'Next Week' was pinned on our room notice board and I saw that at six the next morning, before breakfast, was going to be our first PT session, white PT shirts to be worn, followed with Drill, in barrack dress, after breakfast. At last it was lunchtime, I thought it would never arrive. I was absolutely starving. We were then told that we had the afternoon to sort ourselves out get all of our clothing and equipment cleaned and pressed ready for inspection at 5 p.m.

The next four hours was a hive of activity with only one ironing board and one iron to share between the whole room. It was going to be impossible to get all our clothing pressed and ironed in time. Peter of course had his own. He seemed to have adopted me as someone who needs looking after so I got to share his iron with him. Blanco was a powdery substance with which to clean all your webbing with and had to be applied wet and the equipment allowed to dry. We then needed to clean all the brass buckles with brasso to ensure that they were gleaming.

Needless to say, the blanco and brasso got everywhere and I appeared to have more over my arms, hands and face than I did on the webbing and buckles themselves. We would all have to shower and get spruced up ready for inspection.

At about half four, with everything done as best I could, I took out my little hand towel. Then remembering I now had two nice large green army issue towels I decided to throw it in the bin. "No keep that" said Peter "We can use it as a cleaning rag". He pulled his suitcase out from under his bed and opened it up to reveal a treasure trove.

"Want to borrow a couple of these?" he asked and picked up a couple of flannels from the half dozen or so he had.

"Wouldn't mind" I replied and he handed them over.

There were five showers and three baths to share between the seventy odd recruits and therefore we had to double and triple up under the showers in order to all get through the showers in time. I had never been in a shower before, never mind having to have to share one with a couple of other guys. I found the whole experience very, very embarrassing, keeping my head up and keeping my eyes fixed on the showerhead the whole time.

It goes without saying that the five o'clock inspection was a complete nightmare with the Sgt and Cpl going through everything with a fine toothcomb. The Sgt gave me a particular hard time for not having a razor! When they had entered the room, it looked, to us, that we had done a pretty good job considering the amount of ironing and cleaning we had had to do. But of course, that was wishful thinking. Both Sgt and Cpl flew into a rage and threw our clothing and equipment all over the room in disgust. We would have a hard job sorting out whose was whose when it was all over.

I must admit that considering the windowlene incident I got off fairly lightly compared to some of the others. One poor lad, four beds down, let his anger get the better of him and with tears of rage tried to give as good as he got. He finished up sitting on his bed, head in hands sobbing his poor little heart out when they left.

We rallied around, patting him on the back and saying "Don't let the bastards grind you down - they are bound to give us hell the first few days"

"The first few weeks you mean" someone remarked behind me "they're trying to sort out the men from the boys!"

At six, we went for our evening meal and then worked through until after midnight getting our own and each other's kit in order for the morning. I remember collapsing on the bed exhausted. I must have gone out like a light because when I regained consciousness it was day two.

Chapter 4
TOTAL EXHAUSTION

We were beginning to learn our lesson because most of the men in the room were up and out of bed before reveille. Before the Cpl arrived. However, he still arrived in the normal manner, shouting the familiar "Hands off cocks on with . . . . . "Strutting around the room, his stick tucked under his arm. He was telling us to be ready in fifteen minutes to parade outside in white PT vests and blue shorts ready for our first PT session. About midway down the room, on the opposite side to myself, he stopped to berate one of the lads who were putting the finishing touches to his bed pack.

"Call that square," he bellowed. The hapless lad stood back, head cocked to one side.

"Looks OK!" He dared to say, patting the side nearest to him in an effort to correct a slight lean to the right. The Cpl began to hit the side of the pack with his stick moving upward and along the top.

"Its crap" shouted the Cpl. Then picking the pack up he shook it along the bed undoing the not so tightly wrapped bedcover and spilling blankets and sheets across the bed.

"You will have to try harder Heath my lad".

"Yes, Cpl" replied the lad, looking downhearted.

The Cpl was about to move on up the room when he suddenly stopped and took a pace or two backward. He leaned over the bed. Then pointing his stick at one of the sheets said.

"What's this lad?"

The unfortunate fellow leaned over the bed and peered at the sheet close to the end of the Cpls stick. "Dunno Cpl!" He replied.

"What you mean? You dunno!" shouted the Cpl.

"Dunno Cpl", he said again looking decidedly uncomfortable.

The Cpl lifted the sheet up on the end of his stick and trailing it along the floor moved on to the next man. "You know what this is Smith?" He asked.

"No Cpl". He moved on to the next man.

"Do you know what this is Davies?" he bellowed thrusting the point of his stick under the man's nose.

"Looks like a spunk stain Cpl" he replied.

The Cpl walked backwards to Smith.

"Do you think that is what it is Smith?"

"Yes, Cpl".

"Well why didn't you say so you moron!" he shouted.

He then moved back to Heath.

"Is that what this is Heath, a spunk stain, what have you been doing to yourself?"

Heaths face had turned crimson and he gazed up at the ceiling to avoid having to look the Cpl or any of us in the face.

"Nothing, Cpl" the poor lad shouted.

"Stains like these don't appear from nothing Heath" the Cpl shouted back, then changing tack asked "Who does this sheet belong to Heath?"

"The Army?" replied Heath in a questioning voice.

"You and this bloody sheet belongs to Her Majesty the Queen, Heath".

"Yes, Cpl".

"Who does it belong to Heath?" the Cpl asked again, shaking the sheet under his nose.

"Her Majesty the Queen, Cpl".

"What do you think Her Majesty would say if she found out that you were wankin all over her nice new best cotton sheets?" The Cpl asked.

There was a snigger at this from someone behind the Cpl.

"Oh" he screamed turning around "You all think this is funny do you?"

There was total silence. You could hear a pin drop.

"Well if you all think this is so funny" he said very quietly, and then almost whispering went on.

"I think it would be a good idea for me to inspect all your sheets tomorrow morning" and then he bellowed "and if I find so much as a hint of a single solitary stain I will make all your lives miserable - for ever." He placed the offending sheet over the head of the totally miserable Heath. "Right outside, three ranks, five minutes" and stormed out.

Five minutes later, we were all outside in our three ranks fanning our arms and jumping up and down in a futile attempt to keep warm.

The Cpl appeared.

"Attention", move to the right in threes, right turn!"

We turned to the right.

"By the front, quick march!" And we moved off.

We had barely taken half a dozen steps when he called out.

"By the front, Double March" and we all broke into a feeble trot.

The Cpl moved abreast of the 'Right Hand Man' at the front and increased the pace. "Come on, keep up, stay with me," he urged.

I could see that we were headed toward the football pitch on the other side of the camp. It was roughly a mile. By the time we were half way there our Section had begun to string out and gaps between the ranks expanded noticeably. Luckily, I was very near the front when we moved off. At the halfway point I was much nearer the back. Those who were stronger and fitter than I were overtaking me every few paces.

By the time I reached the football pitch the whole Section was already there running on the spot. I had been about twenty-five yards behind everyone else.

"Come on Houghton" the Cpl, screamed at me "get a move on!"

I caught up and rejoining the section making a feeble effort to run on the spot but I was totally out of breath and trying desperately to suck in air.

"Section, Halt!"

"Whew! Thank Christ!" I thought bending and placing hands on my knees.

It was a very, very brief respite.

"On your faces! Down!" The Cpl shouted and we all dropped face down to the ground. "Twenty press-ups begin!"

The Cpl did his twenty press-ups before the rest of us had got to five.

I am not sure I managed to do a single one successfully. The Cpl came over to me and taking hold of my belt and putting his boot on my bum hauled me up and down rapidly calling "One, two, three, four . . ." and when he got to twenty dropped me like a rag doll onto the grass.

There followed another half hour of agonizing exercises, which left my arms, legs and back trembling and painfully weak. When we fell back into our ranks for the run back to our Spider I could barely lift my feet off the ground. I arrived back at the Spider a good ten minutes after everyone else. I stood soaked in sweat, hands on hips, knees sagging, gasping for breath before a very angry looking Cpl.

"You are going to have to do something about your fitness Houghton and fast" he shouted, "because if you don't Houghton you are going to find yourself down the road so fast you won't have time to blink"

"Yes, Cpl" I gasped. Turning away, the Cpl said

"I got more strength in my dick than you have in your whole body!"

At breakfast, I ate like a horse and even dared, as Oliver did, to return to the hotplate for seconds. The Chef gave me a balling out telling me that if everyone wanted seconds he would have to cook 24 hours a day. Again, my new friend Peter stepped in.

"Come on Chef" he said "the poor lads skin and bone, needs fattening up, you should consider it a challenge". The Chef made no reply, but looking me up and down with a look of utter disdain, plonked another slice of fried bread on my plate topped with a large scoop of scrambled egg.

Back in our room, we changed into Barrack Dress ready for an hours square bashing. Half way through this session of drill, Sgt Steel called me out.

"What happened to you this morning Houghton?" he asked.

"Nothing Sgt! Just felt a bit under the weather," I explained.

"You failed to reach the bare minimum this morning" Sgt Steel told me,

"You will need to toughen up".

"I will Sgt!" I said, "Just need a little time"

I felt close to tears and terrified he would have me kicked out.

"Give me a chance Sgt", I said, "that's all I am asking".

"You are quite famous, Houghton" he told me.

"Who me?" I said surprised.

"Yes, You!"

"Why's that, Sgt?"

"You are known all over the camp as 'The Windowlene Man'"

I could not help myself and actually laughed at that.

"Well Sgt", I said "I done something right then!"

He laughed too, and then told me.

"We will be keeping a very close eye on you Houghton" he said, "and I'm going to be very generous,

I am going to give you the rest of this week and all of next week. If you fail to show a significant improvement by the end of next week then we will have to consider your future in the Army. That clear?"

"Yes, Sgt" I said feeling and looking totally abjectly miserable.

The Sgt patted me on the back.

"You can do it Houghton, keeping trying hard, and never give up!"

"I won't Sgt, I won't".

"That's my boy, off you go."

That lunch time all the lads wanted to know what the Sgt wanted with me. I tried to bluff it out and make excuses but I think most of them guessed I had received a warning.

"Tomorrow," Peter told me "run alongside me, I'll see you through".

"Thanks Pete" I told him.

That afternoon there were three sessions of classroom work, basic map reading, military symbols and how to strip, clean and reassemble a .303 rifle followed by a final session of drill on the parade ground. By the time dinnertime arrived, I had cheered up quite a bit. I felt that I had done well in the classroom and that it would stand me in good stead.

That evening was rather comical. With everyone in the room taking their sheets down to the washrooms for a little extra laundering. This was in anticipation of having to have them publicly inspected the following morning. Even though this was only our second full day together in Room 1, Spider 10, I could sense that there was a definite sense of 'we're in this together' comradeship developing. We were getting to know each other and were chatting away happily. We were less afraid to ask each other to help. Some were better at making bed packs and some were better at Blancoing their equipment and some could wield an iron as good as Old Mother Riley. I had never used an electric iron in my life. On the very rare occasion of having used an iron, it was a cast iron flat iron that had to be placed on the fire or gas stove.

Several lads had bought a new iron so we had more to go round. We all bought a spare razor, brush, soap container and toothbrush in order that we could put those out for inspection and hide the ones we used in our 'private drawer'.

Peter took me along to the gymnasium at about eight o'clock. He taught me to run a hundred yards or so, walk for about fifty, then run another hundred yards and so on. Surprise, surprise, it seemed to work because it I did seem to get there less exhausted. Inside we ran around for a bit and he had me doing leg lifts and other small exercises. I even managed three or four press-ups without collapsing. A vast improvement on the effort I made this mornings.

Peter encouraged me to do this every day and twice on Saturday and Sunday and that he would come with me. Back in our room, Peter had found out that, the room next door had a transistor radio and that he had asked the Cpl if we were allowed one in the room. It turns out we could, so long as it was put away during the day.

Peter telephoned his father and asked him to drop his off at the guardroom over the weekend. Apparently, Peter's home was a short forty minutes drive away.

Having had to wash our sheets that evening and then to iron them dry before making our beds it had pushed our conservancy routine back a good hour. Most of us did not finish getting the various pieces of kit ready for following day's activities until gone one o'clock.

Heath had cheered up after his morning humiliation at the hands of the Cpl. He had been rather quiet up until this evening but he turned out to be quite a comedian. He seemed to have an endless repertoire of jokes, most of them disgustingly rude but they were hilariously funny.

He was also a great mimic and could take off the Sgt's and Cpl's voices off to a 'T'.

One of the lads had received a parcel from home, which had included fruitcake and biscuits, and in no time we had the kettle boiling and we sat around stuffing ourselves listening to Heath and his jokes Our newfound camaraderie cost us another hour of precious sleep and it was after two when someone shouted "Bloody 'ell, its after two o'clock" and almost reluctantly, we all went to bed.

One thing I did notice was that practically everyone took that little extra something to bed with them that night. Either a piece of toilet roll, tissue, or if you was posh like Peter a silk handkerchief!

Chapter 5
PINS AND NEEDLES

Our third day, Wednesday. The Cpl breezed in at five-thirty looking very cheerful.

"Rise and Shine, up and at 'em," he hollers.

We were up and ready. We were dismayed to hear the pounding of rain on the windows as we stood around in our red PT Vests and blue shorts. The Cpl did his usual rounds inspecting the kit laid out on our beds and the contents of several lockers. Was he mellowing a little? He did not carry out the sheet inspection he had threatened to do the day before. I supposed he had heard about our extra laundry the night before and had had his little bit of fun. We were pleased to hear that, because the weather was so bad, we would have use of the gymnasium. However, on our run down from Spider 10 to the gymnasium we still got soaked to the skin.

We spent the first ten minutes inside the gymnasium setting ourselves up what you could call an indoor assault course. We placed out beams, wooden horses, rope obstacles, medicine balls and exercise mats. We then split up into four teams and each team started the 'assault course' at a corner of the gymnasium. Then at a blow of the whistle off we went. My team's first exercise was throwing huge great medicine balls at one another. I could scarcely lift the damn things never mind throw them or catch them. Each one knocked me backward a couple of feet as I caught it. I would then take a deep breath and try to throw it across to the next man.

The first couple of times I was OK but my arms began to tire and ache rapidly and I could barely throw the medicine ball at all, they weighed a ton! Next came the ropes! The best I could manage with those was to hold on tightly and lift my feet off the floor, there was no way I could climb to the top, touch the cross beams close to the ceiling and come down.

The Cpl came along and putting his hands on my arse pushed me up the rope as far as he could reach. There I hung for a minute or two before the whistle went and we had to move round again. The pull-up beams followed and yet again all I could manage was grabbing hold and dangling underneath straining to bend my arms so much as an inch.

By the time we had gone round each obstacle once I was as totally exhausted as I had been the previous day. I was fully expecting a balling out by the Cpl. To my surprise, during our two-minute rest with hands on hips and taking deep breathing exercises, he came up behind me and whispered.

"You're doing well my boy, if I see you doing your damn best, I am happy"

"Thank you Cpl" I told him "I will".

After that little verbal moral boost the Cpl had given me the second time around the gymnasium did not seem quite as hard. I do not think I did any better. But the thing is - I *felt* better'. When we left the gymnasium to return to the Spider I also managed to stay with the group even though the Cpl made us sprint the last hundred yards.

At breakfast, the Chef who had been challenged by Peter the day before to feed me up appeared to have accepted the challenge. Instead of one tablespoon of beans and tomatoes I got two of each, I also received an extra egg! Happy days are here again!

Our drill sessions were also moved from the parade ground to two large 'drill sheds' behind the cookhouse. There we practiced the left, right and about turns till we were dizzy. Following the drill we were back to the classroom for more map reading, map marking, and weapon training. This took us up to lunchtime. After lunch the whole afternoon was taken up with something called 'PULHHEEMS' (*a military term for a complete medical*). When questioned about them the Cpl would tell us wait and see. Everyone seemed to be bright and cheerful and in good spirits at lunchtime. So all in all it had been a good day so far. If only we had known!

After lunch we paraded outside and were marched away in a totally new direction. We were marched down towards and then past the main gate and guardroom, then along past the Cpls' Mess, The Sgt's Mess and then the Officers' Mess and then, there it was, a huge building, called the 'Station Medical Centre'. Very soon we were all held in a large reception room. Stands had been strategically placed so that we moved in a great circle cubicle to cubicle. Shortly after we were told to strip down to our underwear and leave our clothes on our chairs. I was embarrassed to find that I was the only one I could see actually wearing army issue underwear nicknamed 'Jungle Greens'.

Then things really started to move. We had to march around in threes. First one was that embarrassing cold hands and "cough" routine again, after which we were told to bend over so that they could look at our arse's. I was too young and naive to know why! Next cubicle was the eye tests. Where upon the doctor remarked "Excellent, excellent 1 over 1" which meant I assumed I had excellent eyesight. I had the same result in my hearing tests, "Good, Excellent, Well done!" The only adverse remarks were again about my height and weight. Having had our bodies checked from top to toe we moved down to an enclosed area marked 'Grouping and Immunization'!

"Is that what I think it means?" I asked Hutton a member of my three.

"You mean a jab?"

"Yeah! Are we going to have a jab?"

"Looks that way," said Smith, the third man.

We jostled each other for a bit to see who we could get to go first but once inside the enclosed area we found that there was a bit of a queue anyway. We could see down the line that the first desk we would come to was jabbing thumbs with scalpels and taking blood samples. A medical orderly told us to gently massage our thumbs to ease the blood flow and make the taking of a sample easier. A little further we saw the inoculations being given! Jesus Christ! I had never seen such big needles. The last time I remember having an injection of any kind was when I was about seven or eight years old. I had complained to my Mom for several days that my knees hurt!

This was a cunning plan of mine to avoid the school sports day on the Friday. There was a lot of Polio around at the time and so finally, as a precaution, she took me to the doctors on the Thursday morning. The doctor after questioning me for a while, checking my reflexes, took out a huge needle, which, my Mom told me later, only contained water! As soon as the doctor approached me with the needle I declared the pain all gone and my knees miraculously cured. However the doctor had insisted in giving me the injection in my left buttock. He probably only inserted it a millimetre! He then asked how my left leg felt and did I think I needed one in my right buttock for my right knee. "Oh no my right knee was fine!" I declared fearfully. I never tried to skive off school again! Back to the Medical Centre.

As we moved forward I could see Hutton was as white as a sheet. Poor Hutton was the proud owner of one of the ugliest and crookedest noses I have ever seen. He told me that when he was little he had gone to watch his father playing cricket and had wondered a bit too far towards the green. To cut a long story short, he was hit smack on the nose with a hit that should have gone over the boundary, had it not made contact with his nose, splitting it in two and breaking his cheek bone to boot. The shorter the queue got the whiter and more nervous Hutton got. Not that I was immune to such terror either, because I was wringing my hands and massaging my thumbs like there was no tomorrow. Then it was Hutton's turn. The medic took his hand and with a swift jab pierced his thumb. Nothing.

He squeezed the thumb. The tiniest blob you could possibly imagine appeared. The medic had another go and jabbed him again. Unfortunately for poor old Hutton the medic gave up on that thumb and tried the other one on his right hand. He was more successful this time. I realized then that it was because Hutton was left handed and had been massaging his right thumb all along! The medic had been working on, and trying to extract blood from the thumb on his left hand!

Watching this display I was wringing my hands and squeezing both thumbs as hard as I could. As Hutton moved forward for the jab in his left arm I moved forward, facing away from the medic, to have my thumb sliced open. I was suddenly and urgently in need of a pee! The medic took hold of my thumb and gave it a quick jab. Splat! "Shit!" I heard the medic cry out. I turned towards him and saw that there was a nice neat straight line of blood stretching from right side of his glasses, down across his nose and cheek, and onto his nice white collar and jacket.

"You might not have any meat on you" he said "but you've certainly got enough blood!"

I heard a bellow of laughter from the lads in the queue behind.

"Good on yer Ricky!" Someone shouted

"One in the eye for 125 Training Party!"

"Bloody serves 'em right" called another.

By this time Hutton had received his first jab and was moving unsteadily forward to receive the next one to be given in his right arm. That medic asked if he was alright and he nodded.

I was being given my first jab as I watched Hutton take his second. Hutton done - he took a pace forward. Then wallop! He went out like a light falling flat on his face. Unfortunately for Hutton his chin came into contact with the corner of metal medical trolley splitting it wide open. Blood was everywhere. They lifted him up and carried him off to a side room to recover.

I was totally unnerved by this and was visibly shaking as I moved up for my first jab. To top it all, I could see that the medic had been shocked by Hutton's nose dive too and as he approached me with this nine inch needle I could see that the needle he was holding was also shaking uncontrollably. The medic gripped my arm and tried unsuccessfully to find any real muscle in which to plunge his needle. In the end he just squeezed and bunched as much skin as he could get between his thumb and forefinger together, which wasn't much, and plunged his needle home.

Unfortunately for me when he pressed the plunger he realized the point had come out the other side of the bunch of skin and he had to retract the needle an inch and try again. When he had done he turned to the chap who was to give me the second jab and said "Got your work cut out with this one! There's nothing to stick the needle in to!"

By the time we got back to the Spider, Hutton had been brought back and laid on his bed; he still looked pale and a little sheepish!

"Dunno what happened there," he said.

"Don't worry about it!" Heath remarked, "Now your chin matches your nose!"

To which we all, including Hutton, had a good laugh. When I took my shirt off, where my injections had been given, my arms had swollen more than just a little.

"Yeah! Look! They've injected a bit of muscle into Houghton!" Smith told everyone.

Everyone started to remove their shirts and inspect the areas they had been injected but I am proud to say none of them had swellings like mine!

Later that evening Peter had a message that a parcel had been dropped off for him at the guardroom. "Ah! must be what I asked Father for!" he said. He asked me to walk down the guardroom with him and off we went.

"Remember" asked Peter "I told you I have a younger brother, Michael"

"Yeah" I replied.

"Well Michael is fourteen, but he's big for his age, about your size". Peter told me.

"Is he?" I said, wondering what this was leading up to.

"I'll show you," said Peter.

At the guardroom Peter received his parcel. It was quite big. Bigger than the size of a transistor radio.

"What you got in there?" I asked him.

"Don't be offended will your Ricky?" said Peter. He genuinely looked concerned.

"Why should I be offended?" I asked.

"Well" said Peter hesitantly, "I asked Father to include a bit more than the transistor"

"Like what?" I asked.

We sat on the steps of our Spider and Peter unwrapped his parcel. Inside there were three pairs of Y-Fronts, three pairs of socks, two shirts, a lovely Grey v-necked pullover, a pair of grey slacks and a pair of size eight brogue brown shoes.

In the middle of all this was the transistor radio. I looked at the clothes with no comprehension of what Peter was on about.

"These were Michael's," he told me.

"Oh" I said, still not understanding the significance of what Pete was saying.

"I thought you might like them," said Peter hesitantly. "No-one need know".

The penny dropped. I was so touched by Peter's generosity I was stumped for words.

"Sorry", said Peter, mistaking my silence as offence, "but they would probably have finished up at the village hall at a charity sale anyway".

"I'm not offended mate" I said, finally finding my voice. "I'm chuffed to bits, don't know what to say!"

"You don't have to say anything" Peter replied. "I would be just pleased if you would accept them!"

"Would I ever!" I exclaimed. Keeping hold of the transistor radio, Peter handed me the parcel and we went inside.

"Hey fellahs! Peter called out as we entered the room. "Me and Ricky here just got a parcel each of home"

"What you got Peter?" Heath asked.

"The transistor radio" Peter declared.

"And you Ricky" Heath asked again.

"Nothing much" I said "Just a bit of clobber is all".

Realizing there were no goodies such as fruitcake or biscuit's the others in the room quickly lost interest and I reverently placed my new clothes in my army suitcase under the bed.

"Thank you! Peter" I told him. I could not wait to try them on!

"Pleasure is all mine old bean" he replied.

Chapter 6
HALT, WHO GOES THERE!

I woke on Thursday morning to a buzz of excitement.

"Ave you read Part One Orders?" Peter asked me as I sat up rubbing my eyes.

"No, just got up, why?"

"It says 125 Training Party are on guard Friday, Saturday and Sunday" he replied excitedly.

"We can't all be on guard", I said "Its only a twelve man guard".

"Yeah, I know, but the Cpl said it's our room on Friday".

During the day the Provost Sgt and his men guard the barracks but at night the guard is taken over by the trainees from six p.m. until six a.m.

"How do we know who's on guard and who is not?" I asked Peter.

"Cpl said he would put up the list after breakfast" he answered.

The Cpl turned up a minute or two later, minus his list, and we had to wait until after our morning PT to find out who the lucky dozen would be. Our PT this morning was a straight three-mile speed march, (running for a couple of hundred yards and then walking). It would be the furthest I had ever run. Peter and I had been running to and from the gymnasium the last couple of nights as well as our normal PT in the mornings. That day I surprised myself. I did lag behind a little at times, but always managed to catch up during the walks.

By the time we got back after our run I had managed to stay with the group. Gasping for breath and exhausted, but I had done it. I had managed to complete the three miles. I got a pat on the back from the Cpl as we fell out to get showered and changed for breakfast. Even one or two of the lads felt obliged to comment and to congratulate me on my success. As sure as eggs are eggs. When we got back from breakfast and read the list of names for the guard duty on Friday, my name was on it. I was disappointed to find my best mate Peter was not there.

We had been smothering the toes and heels of our best boots in polish and setting fire to them to remove the dimples so that we could polish, bull them up, to a very high shine. We hadn't realized we would need them quite so soon. That morning after breakfast we drew our rifles from the armoury to train with them for the first time. Mine was Butt No 17. That day we learned to 'shoulder' and 'present' arms and how to march around with them. We all felt particularly proud as we got used to moving around carrying our 7.62 Self Loading Rifles. I hadn't anticipated just how heavy they were and my wrist, arm and shoulder was aching like hell by lunchtime.

I also received a second boost to my moral that Thursday. When Peter and I went to the NAAFI for our tea break and I went into the toilets to put a penny in scales I found that I had put on three or four pounds in weight since Tuesday. Things were looking up.

Thursday night was spent ironing our uniforms and bulling our boots in preparation for the guard duty the next day. We were warned that if our kit were not up to scratch we would find ourselves on guard again on Sunday night.

We carried out a dress rehearsal that night with Peter acting the part of the Party Officer. He carried his cameo role off to a T to the great amusement of us all. He was quite thorough and it's probably thanks to him that none of use received more than fairly mild criticism.

For PT on Friday we were once again in the gymnasium to carry out circuit training. I astounded myself by managing no less than five press-ups and ten sit-ups. Also, to a resounding cheer from my mates around me, and with the encouragement of the Cpl screaming "Up up, go on Houghton, nearly there!" I managed to get my chin over the bar in the pulls ups for the first time. Even though I only managed the one I felt a great sense of achievement. I knew I still had a long way to go but for the first time I was gaining in confidence and was sure that by the end of the next week I would have reached the standard of fitness I needed.

As Friday progressed I became more and more excited about the Guard Duty and looked forward to it eagerly. Some of my mates were critical of my enthusiasm saying that I was "Barmy, who in their right mind looks forward to a night on guard" but I just couldn't help it. I kept checking the time and wishing the day would pass more quickly.

Obviously the more I looked at the time the more the time seemed to drag by. At last five-thirty arrived and we were paraded by our Cpl. He gave us a fairly thorough inspection, giving me a balling out for fluff on my beret, and then he marched us down to the guard room.

We were to carry out four duties, man the barrier at the front gate, patrol the camp perimeter, patrol the camp itself and patrol the ammunition and armoury compound. We had to carry out two shifts during the night from six p.m. onwards. Those not out on patrol would have to carry out conservancy inside the guardroom itself, polishing the floor, dusting and cleaning windows. I was one of the three on first patrol. I was to patrol the camp perimeter, which meant my other shift would be from midnight until two a.m.

I was briefed to watch out for recruits trying to sneak out of the camp or for anyone trying to enter the camp illegally. I was given a large police whistle to use if needed and a large pickaxe handle in lieu of a rifle. I was told to report in to the guardroom every half hour. I still didn't have a watch of my own and had to borrow one from Heath who would be taking over from me at eight p.m. Having walked around the camp perimeter fence a couple of times I realized that being on guard was not all what it was cracked up to be. The second hour of my two-hour shift seemed to take forever and I could not wait to get back inside the guardroom for a 'well earned' mug of tea.

At nine o'clock a box of corn beef and cheese sandwiches were delivered which were demolished in two minutes flat. The Cpl put a few aside for those out on patrol. My hunger satisfied, I lay on the bed for a couple of hour's kip, before my second shift. I must have slept because the next thing I knew I was being shaken awake by one of the lads who shoved a mug of tea in my hand. "Your stag in fifteen minutes" he told me.

I got up and prepared myself to go out into the night. I had thought I would do the same thing as before, patrolling the perimeter fence, but no the Cpl called me over.

"You are in the ammunition and armoury compound," he told me.

"Right, Cpl".

"Now listen carefully," he said. "The compound has been broken into twice over the last twenty years, once by the IRA".

"Right, Cpl".

"Now at the gate to the compound, on the left, there is the alarm bell, you hear anything suspicious or see anyone trying to break in you ring that alarm, understood?"

"Yes, Cpl!"

"Now when you get into the compound, press the alarm, and I will switch it off from here, that way I know you know were the alarm bell is, OK?"

"Yes, Cpl!"

"OK, lad, off you go, don't forget your pick axe handle " he said "you will be relieved at two o'clock, and don't forget what I told you!"

"Ok, I won't Cpl"

I left the guardroom and walked around the side to the compound. The whole area of the compound gate was floodlit. The lad I was relieving took out the key, removed the huge padlock, and opened the gate and handed me the key. "Don't forget to lock the padlock" he told me and rushed off thankful his stag was over and done with. I padlocked the gate, put the key in my breast pocket, and went off to explore the compound, tapping the toe of my boot with the metal end of my pickaxe handle.

There were two wedge shaped entrances to underground bunkers, a bit like air raid shelters, which is where, I assumed, they kept the ammunition. The armoury itself was a long wooden building with great bars on the windows, horizontally and vertically, I couldn't imagine anyone getting into the building without making a lot of noise.

After a while, and beginning to feel the cold, I made my way onto the balcony of the armoury and stood there out of the wind. I had to pick up the field telephone every half hour and turning the little handle report all is well to the Cpl in the guardroom. I did this at half past twelve and then had another wander around to keep warm. A few minutes later I was back on the balcony whistling quietly to myself. At one o'clock I did the same, a walk around the compound, once again tapping the toe of my boot with the metal end of my pickaxe handle, as I went. Back on the balcony, having reported in, I leaned against the wall to wait, rubbing my hands to warm them from the chilling wind. Then I heard this funny noise!

On hearing the noise I moved quietly off the balcony trying to determine where the noise was coming from. Tiptoeing to the corner of the building I peered around to see a man pushing his way under the metal fencing. I was just about to run to the gate to ring the alarm when I suddenly realized that, by doing so, I would be running into the floodlit area. Without a doubt he would see me and scarper. I paced in a circle for a minute fretting, debating what to do. If I used my whistle he would hear it, and if I tried to make my way to the gate to ring the alarm he would see me.

I took a second look. He was in under the fence to his waist, squirming his way through not fifteen yards away. "Right you bastard" I thought gritting my teeth "You're not getting in here while I'm around".

Heart pounding with fear I suddenly ran out from the balcony screaming as I went.

"AAAAAArghh!"

In seconds I was standing over the man, eyes tightly shut, smacking him over the head with the metal end of my pickaxe handle for all I was worth. He brought his hands up over his head to try to protect himself. When I saw him do this it just made me whack him even harder determined to render him unconscious before he managed to escape.

"Stop! Stop! What are you doing you lunatic! Stop!" It was Lt Mortimer.

I stopped. Heart pounding, breathless. Lt Mortimer came running up out of the darkness.

"What are you doing?" he shouted at me once more.

"He was trying to break in," I explained.

By this time the man was struggling back the way he had come.

"You were supposed to ring the alarm!" shouted Lt Mortimer.

"Why on earth did you not ring the alarm?"

The man was sitting, back against the fence, moaning and rubbing his head.

"If I came out from the balcony into the flood lit area he would have seen me" I said

"You must ring the alarm," he moaned, exasperated

"Ring the damn alarm!" he shouted!

I ran over to the alarm and rang it and within minutes the whole guard was running toward the compound. The Cpl ready with his padlock key. The man I had tried to render unconscious finally managed to regain his feet. There was a trickle of blood running down the side of his face. It was the Provost Sgt. The man who had been at the window when I first arrived. The man who had threatened to rip my arm off if I knocked on his door again!

"Why didn't you ring the bloody alarm!" he asked me. "I thought if I came out into the flood lights you would see me and escape," I explained for the second time.

Less panicked now, seeing the Provost Sgt on his feet, Lt Mortimer just said, "Next time, just ring the alarm bell". Then "Its you!" he said in a surprised voice "Its you, the windowlene man!"

"Yes, Sir" I said hanging my head.

"I should have known" he said, "You realize you will be charged for tonight's little escapade don't you my lad".

"Yes, Sir", I replied.

"Back to the guard room you!" the Cpl ordered. The Lt took the Provost Sgt by the arm and led him off in the general direction of the Medical Centre. I made my way back to the guardroom. Once inside I noticed a little blood and a few Grey hairs stuck to the metal end of my pickaxe handle and wiped it off with my sleeve.

That Saturday morning at nine o'clock I was ordered to report to the Squadron HQ. The Squadron HQ was hallowed ground. None of us had ever been near it thus far. At the Sqn HQ by a huge Sgt Major sporting a large handle bar moustache. There were two other soldiers with him. "Houghton?" he asked. "Stand there, between these two men".

I went to stand between the men as ordered.

"You are to be charged with two charges" the Sgt Major told me "First Charge" He went on "Disobeying a lawful command contrary to section 55 of the Army Act 1955, in that you, at Cove, Farnborough, when ordered to ring the Alarm at the Ammunition and Armoury compound, in the event of an incident. Failed to do so" He looked me up and down "Do you understand the charge?"

"Yes, Sir" I said, though I hadn't got a clue what he was on about.

"Second Charge" he went on "Conduct to the prejudice of good order and military discipline contrary to section 69 of the Army Act 1955 in that you at Cove,

Farnborough, did assault Sgt Rogers with a pick axe handle, do you understand the charge?"

Yes, Sir".

At that moment the said Sgt Rogers appeared. His head was heavily bandaged and his beret perched precariously on top. He simply glared at me.

The Sgt Major opened the door to the Squadron Office. "Escort, Witness and Accused, Attention!" be bellowed. "By the front, right wheel, quick march!" We marched into the Squadron Office, straight through and into the Officer Commanding office.

"Left wheel, mark time, halt." Shouted the Warrant Officer.

"Escort, Witness and Accused! Left Turn!" We turned and I found myself standing in front of a Major.

"Are you?" he asked reading out my number, rank and name".

"Yes, Sir" I replied.

He read out the charges to me again.

"Do you understand the charges?" He asked me

"Yes, Sir" I replied.

The Major asked the witness, the Provost Sgt, to give his statement. He reported that "at 01.15 on Saturday he was attempting to enter the compound to test the alertness and efficiency of the guard when he was assaulted by Sapper Houghton with the metal end of a Pick Axe handle causing him actual bodily harm".

"What do you have to say for yourself?" asked the Major.

Again I explained about the flood lighting and that if I moved to the gate to ring the alarm any intruder would have seen me and might have made good his escape"

"Hmmm" said the Major mulling over what I told him.

"Would you accept my punishment or do you elect to be tried by Courts Martial?" He asked me.

*Bloody Hell!" I thought to myself "I'm in for it now".

"On the first charge" he said, " I find you guilty "On the second charge I find you Not Guilty"

"Thank you, Sir" I said in a quiet voice

"Shut Up!" screamed the Warrant Officer "Don't speak unless you're spoken to!" The Major looked up at me, then at the Provost Sgt, then back at me and with half a smile on his face said "I fine you two shillings, march him out Sgt Major"

We did the attention, right turn, quick march, and back out of the Squadron Office.

"Think yourself lucky" the Sgt Major told me. "Fall out".

When I got back to Spider 10 I was greeted with a hero's welcome by the lads in my room all eager to hear what had happened and how I'd got on. On hearing the commotion Sgt Steel came to our room.

"Ah, Houghton my lad". he said "Lt Mortimer would like a quick word with you".

I followed him out of the room down the 'Troop Office' where Lt Mortimer sat at his desk looking slightly worried.

"Houghton" he said, "What is the matter with you lad?"

"Nothing, Sir" I replied.

"Disaster seems to follow you around" he said "First the windowlene! And now this!"

"Sorry, Sir" I said, fearing he was going to give me another warning.

"I don't know what to do about you Houghton" he went on "But I am pleased with the way you have improved these last few days, I can see you are really trying hard".

"Thank you, Sir!" I said.

"Please, Houghton!" he said in a pleading voice "No more incidents eh?"

"No, Sir" I said.

"Off you go then!"

Sgt Steel took me back outside the office and said

"You have a new knick name Houghton!"

"Oh?" I replied, "What's that?"

"Yeah" he told me "its Wam Bam The Windowlene Man!" and he walked off chuckling to himself.

Chapter 7
SECONDS OUT! DING DING!

When I was at school, about eleven, there was this estate and school bully called 'Bull'. Usually Bull left me alone. This was probably because he knew that if word got to either of my brothers Don and Kev that he had been giving me a hard time they would come looking for him. Two or three other lesser bullies usually accompanied Bull in order to avoid being bullied themselves. Bull also knew I had two good friends, William and Ben. They were no push over. Only his Mother called William, 'William', as you might have guessed. Every one else called him 'Bill'.

You can imagine what my nickname was, being usually flanked by Bill and Ben, you got it! My nickname at that particular school was 'Weed'. Bill lived on the other side of the estate and although Ben only lived a few doors from me the poor lad was off school with the mumps. That particular afternoon, on the way home from school, I caught sight of Bull and his disciples walking down the street towards me. They were in between my home and me. It went against the grain for me to back off and look for a way to avoid them. Besides they had already spotted me and were fanning out across the pavement to block any attempt by me to go around them.

"Hiya Weed, how you doing?" asked Bull

"I'm Ok, Bull" I replied. "You?"

"What you got in your satchel he asked snatching it from me.

"Just school books" I replied and tried to snatch back my satchel.

Bull unfastened my satchel and poured the contents onto the pavement. He sifted through them using his foot creasing and smudging with dirt the covers and pages. He then gave the little pile of books a kick scattering half of them into the road. He picked up what remained and threw them over the nearest garden fence and dropping the satchel at my feet.

"You are the most idiotic ignoramus I have ever met," I told him.

"What you call me," he said, grabbing me by the hair.

"He called you an ignoramus Bull!" one of his disciples told him.

"I would bash him if he called me that" called another.

"Shut your face!" Bull shouted to his disciple "Nobody asked you".

"I don't think I like what you called me Weed!" he growled into my ear. "I dare you to call me it again!"

"You are an ignoramus!" I told him. Bull took hold of my right ear and twisted it viciously. I tried to knock his hand but failed. "Leave off Bull!" I pleaded.

"Or else?" he asked.

"Just leave me in peace will you" I whined.

Bull took a pinch of skin on my neck pinching it between thumb and forefinger and twisted hard. I squealed like a stuck pig. My eyes were watering and my hands gripping his wrist trying to pull his hand away. His followers were shrieking with laughter and doing their utmost to egg him on.

He reached up to the other side of my neck and did the same, pinching and twisting the skin on my neck as hard as he could.

"I'll leave you in peace when I'm good and ready" he said through gritted teeth.

The pain in my neck was excruciating as he gave each side of my neck another twist.

"Please Bull!" I begged.

Bull then leaned back, still gripping my neck, and laughed loudly. His disciples and followers followed suit.

"Give him what for Bull" I heard someone shout.

Suddenly I saw red. White lightning flashes before my eyes. The next thing I knew I was standing over Bull, bent forward, my small fists in a tight ball. I was trembling and shaking uncontrollably. I could not remember, how or what had happened. Bull was holding his nose. There was a slight trickle of blood oozing from his nostrils. He did not look hurt but there was a complete look of sheer astonishment and amazement on his face. His disciples and followers standing around, eyes wide and mouths open in surprise. "Leave me in peace Bull!" I gasped breathlessly, "Just leave me in peace!" I turned and walked away, cringing slightly, fully expecting Bull to attack me from behind. But he didn't.

I never had a run in with Bull again. It would be too much for me to believe that he was now avoiding me. However, the next time I saw him at school, although we never spoke, he raised his hand in greeting and I replied in the same way.

I felt sorry for Bull, I understood 'bullies' as those who were some how inadequate and used their strength to try to compensate for it. It was their only way of seeking the attention they needed. Their way of attracting so called friends. I don't think I ever met a bully who had what you might consider a real friend.

Back in Spider 10 Heath and I decided to pop to the NAAFI for a quick sandwich and a game of pool. Neither of us was any good and had one frame apiece in a best of three frames. We were more than half way through the frame, Heath winning so far, when three lads walked up to pool table.

"Off!" said the middleman who was the taller and larger of the three.

"Off" he said again "games over, I want a game with me mates here".

"Won't be long," I told him leaning over table, "games almost over".

As I went to take my shot he took the end of my cue and pulled it backward spoiling my shot. "When I tell you off! I don't mean in ten minutes, or five minutes or even I minute, I mean now!" the lad told me as he squared up to me the look in his eyes daring me to say no. I did.

"I'm sorry mate", I told him, and "We are going to finish the game, be patient eh!"

The lad walked around the table pushing the remaining balls into the pockets, his friends having a good laugh as he did so,

"As I said", he said "games over!"

He continued around the table until he was again facing me. He was a good head taller than I was and certainly much heavier.

"Oh what a shame" I told him "We were enjoying that game!" He laughed and patted me on the head. "Yeah, shame, now run along little boy!"

"I meant," I told him in as firm a voice as I could muster "it's a shame we have to start the frame again!"

Then turning to Heath I said "and we might even make it best of five eh Heath!" The lad suddenly reached behind my head and gripping me by the hair took a hold on my nose and twisted it viciously. I felt the gristle in my nose crack as he twisted and my eyes began to stream with tears.

"The only best of five you are going to get is one of these," he told me holding his fist up to my face.

"Why don't you leave us in peace you ignoramus" I told him as I tried to push his hand away from my face. He still had a loose hold and taking a firmer grip he gave my nose another vicious twist.

I saw red. White lightning flashes before my eyes. I remembered nothing of the next few seconds. What I do remember was standing over the man. Heath, and one of the other man's cronies were holding me tightly by the arms. I held a broken cue in my hand, the splintered end of which was an inch or two from the man's throat. The lad had a five or six inch red mark down the right side of his temple and a large bruise was beginning to form on his cheek. I was trembling and shaking uncontrollably.

"Why don't you leave us in peace?" I asked him breathlessly "Leave us in peace!"

At that moment the Canteen NCO came running over.

"Oh! What the hell is going on here?" He shouted. He stood looking from me to the lad on the floor hands on hips demanding an answer.

The lad struggled to his feet "Oh nothing", he replied "Bloody tripped over his cue and banged me head on the table".

The Canteen NCO looked unconvinced.

"Names?" He asked us.

"Rigsby" replied the lad "55 ex-Junior Leaders"

"Houghton" I told him "125 Training Party"

"Right, back to your Spiders, I don't want to see either of you in here again" he told us, "and I will be giving a full report to your Troop Sgts." he called after us. He then moved to the circle of onlookers, as the NAAFI had been quite busy, and began questioning those nearest to the pool table. I turned to look for Heath to say "Lets go" but he had already left.

By the time I got back to Spider 10 everyone was fully aware of what had happened. News travels fast in the Army! Heath was breathlessly recounting every second of the fracas. Which couldn't have been much because it was all over in a split second? Heath explained that one minute the lad had a grip on my nose and the next minute I was all over him trying to beat him to death with my snooker cue. An exaggeration if ever I heard one. Heath claimed that had he and the other feller not grabbed me when they did, he was sure I would have done him serious harm, with the splintered end of my cue.

"Our little Ricky", he said, "is a little tiger when he gets going!"

This aspect of the incident was what really frightened me. Twice in my life now I had been involved in a real fight and twice I can remember nothing!

It was not long before the Party Sgt turned up and called me into the office for a dressing down.

"Bloody Hell Houghton" he said, "It was only this morning the Party Officer was telling you no more incidents, what happened?"

I related the incident from beginning to end, as far as I could remember, finishing off with a sincere apology for what had happened.

"This Rigsby is well known as a bit of a hard case" the Sgt told me "a bit of a trouble maker".

"Yes, Sgt!" I replied, head hanging, yet again, in embarrassment and shame.

"I didn't start it, honest Sgt".

"You never cease to astound me, Houghton, he's bloody twice your size, and whatever possessed you to take him on?"

"I don't know, one minute he was pulling my nose, next he was on the floor," I told him.

"Well Houghton this Rigsby is trouble, he will be after you to get even, don't go to the NAAFI on your own and steer clear of him, right?"

"Yes, Sgt".

Then the Sgt laughed "You're amazing, I'd never have believed it possible from you Houghton". I didn't reply, not knowing how to reply. The Sgt led me back to the door of his office. "But that's one in the eye for 55 ex-Junior Leaders eh!" he said patting me on the back "Off you go - and remember, steer clear of Rigsby and his cronies".

"I will" I replied.

I did stay away from the NAAFI for about a week and did see Rigsby a couple of times as we made our way around the Camp. About a week later, absolutely starving, I decided to nip to the NAAFI and grab a quick cheese and onion roll and a coke before it closed. When I got there it was just after half past nine. NAAFI closed at ten. The only people in the NAAFI were Rigsby, the same two who were with him before, and another I had not seen before.

I bought my roll and coke and glancing across saw Rigsby and his mates leaning against the pool table watching me. Although they scared the hell out of me, I could not bring myself just to walk back out, so I walked to the table and sat down, facing Rigsby and his mates, and began to eat my roll. Rigsby was holding his cue in his right hand, patting his left hand with the tip end of the cue. He walked slowly over to my table and stood there for a minute or two just looking down at me. There was still a faint red line on his temple and the bruising on his cheek had not yet fully healed. Our eyes met and held for a second or two, There was a 'who's going to look away first contest'.

"Fancy a game?" he asked suddenly.

"Skint" I told him, "only had enough for my roll and a coke".

"My shout" he said.

"That case, don't mind if I do, mind you I'm crap at pool" I told him.

"You might be crap at pool", he replied, "but you are quite handy with a pool cue!"

I was very suspicious, expecting something, but not knowing what. He fished out a sixpenny piece and inserted into the pool table. Having set up the balls he asked, "You want to break?"

"After you" I told him and he broke off. Potting a red as he did so. He then went on to pot another three.

"Bit short on cue's," he said before handing me the one he had been using.

I managed to pot a couple before Rigsby was back in amongst the balls. He potted the black with a flourish. "Best of three?" He asked. I shrugged and he took out another sixpenny piece. Rigsby was well on the way to winning that frame too but the black went in off right at the end of the game. The third frame was a forgone conclusion, I only managed to pot one ball before Rigsby cleared up.

"Thanks" I told him, "I can see you've played before".

"Once or twice" he told me.

"I'm off, got a bit of kit to sort out yet, thanks for the game" I said.

"Don't mention it" he replied.

Although I did see Rigsby around the camp and in the NAAFI off and on we never engaged in conversation again. We simply acknowledged each other's presence with a simple lifting of the hand or a nod of the head.

Chapter 8
WEEK TWO

The first full weekend went off without further incident. What a difference one week in your life can make. It seemed I had been there for months, not just one week. The morning continued with our pre-breakfast PT sessions. There was a rumour that from week three onwards PT would take place during the last session of the afternoon and if this were true it would mean an extra hour in bed each day. When I returned from breakfast, on Tuesday morning, I was told by Sgt Steel that I had to report to the Medical Officer on Wednesday morning at eleven o'clock, as he wanted to check my weight. That really got me worried and I began to gorge myself with anything that looked the slightest bit edible.

Also Tuesday morning, at NAAFI break time, I was reading Part One Orders on the Troop Notice Board outside the office when I heard the Party Officer and the Sgt discussing one of my room mates Riverton. They always seemed to leave the troop office door half way open for some reason, perhaps so they could hear what was going on in the washrooms, corridors and ablutions, they seemed to not to realize that anyone reading the Notice Board could also hear them!

"I don't know what we are going to do about Riverton," the Officer was saying.

"Difficult one, Sir" replied the Sgt, "Not that he's doing badly, and he's actually doing very well at the moment".

"He's down for driving training in a couple of weeks" went on Lt Mortimer.

"Hmmm, they'll have to cut a hole in the cab roof for his head", laughed the Sgt.

"Seriously though", said Lt Mortimer, "we cannot pair him off with anyone, he's just far too tall, he will not be able to fit in when it comes down to basic combat engineering".

I was the youngest in the room. Riverton was just a few weeks older than I was. But what Riverton lacked in years he certainly made up for in height. He was six foot six if he was an inch and still growing! He had a tangle of fair very curly hair perched on a huge head. He had Prince Charles's ears that stuck out a mile and hands the size of shovels. When in bed his feet stuck out through the bars at the foot of his bed like two fresh leg of lamb ready for the oven. He could pick up a basketball with one hand as easy as I would a tennis ball. The rest of his body was in equal proportion to his height. I can personally vouch for that, having been forced to share a shower with him one day last week, it was like coming face to face with a baby elephant. It was like comparing a cocktail sausage with a cucumber!

Because Riverton's extremities was so far from his brain, his arms and legs appeared to have a mind of their own, lacking totally in any form of coordination. It was quite amusing to watch him walking about. However, we had to be careful not to let him catch us laughing at him. We weren't that bad, we laughed with him rather than at him.

When he marched or ran his arms appeared to go outward and back instead of forward and back. Not that he ran much! When we were out on a run it seemed that all he had to do was open his legs a little more, take a bigger stride, and he could walk while the rest of us jogged along around him his head and shoulders way above the rest of us.

I could understand the Officers' problems. In the gymnasium when they set the bar at the height for the remainder of us to run up to, place our hands on, and jump over. Riverton would casually walk up and step over the damn thing. If we set the pull-up bar at the correct height for Riverton, hardly any of us could reach it! We often joked with Riverton with long tried and tested remarks such as. "Watch out for low flying aircraft mate", "Is it snowing up there!" and if it was misty "Can you see anything through all that cloud"

Another problem for poor Riverton was that whenever we were being brought to attention, or to stand at ease, the rest of us slammed our feet in, in unison with a loud crunch. But Riverton's feet always seemed to hit the ground a second or two after everyone else. Much to the consternation of the Drill Instructor. He did not receive too much abuse from the Training Cpl's because in doing so they would invariably get a crick in the neck. Riverton, though, was well liked because he always mucked in without being asked. He seldom laughed out loud but he would sit on his bed a smile on his face listening to all the banter going on around him.

He was a godsend when it came to the cleaning the windows and dusting the tops of lockers.

"Well, we are going to have to do something soon", the Officer said, "We cannot let matters just drift on".

"What you have in mind?" asked the Sgt.

"He would be ideal for service in the Guards Division, the Coldstream Guards are just down the road in Aldershot".

"Sounds a good idea to me," replied the Sgt "But it will break his little heart, he was dead set on being a Royal Engineer!" I couldn't help fretting about what I had overheard, forgetting my worries about the Medical Officer, and talked with Peter, Heath and a few of the lads about it. We resolved to wait until Wednesday and see what happened.

Wednesday morning arrived and Riverton took part in the PT and joined in with us at breakfast. After breakfast we heard the Cpl tell him that Lt Mortimer wanted a talk with him. The rest of us carried on with a session of rifle drill on the parade ground, which took us up to NAAFI break at ten o'clock. When we returned to the room after the drill session, before going to the NAAFI, Riverton was sitting on the end of his bed looking totally dejected.

"What's up Rivers?" We asked him full knowing what was wrong. "They want to chuck me out!" Riverton moaned close to tears "to some infantry mob down the road".

"No!" we all exclaimed in shock and surprise "Which mob?" "Bloody Coldstream Guards" he replied.

I could see his eyes watering and believe it or not his bottom lip was quivering uncontrollably. He was close to sobbing his heart out!

We all went into our carefully discussed and rehearsed plan of action. Peter looked at me and I got the ball rolling.

"You jammy sod, you!" I declared "some buggers have all the luck!"

"The Coldstream Guards" shouted Heath, I wanted to join the Guards Division but they told me I was two inches too short!"

"Yeah, me too", exclaimed Peter, "Father wanted me in the Guards but I was not tall enough either".

"You are a jammy sod" I told him again. "The Coldstream Guards are the Cavalry, you get a bloody great horse, probably a white stallion, all the best gear, and get to drive a Light Tank to boot".

Riverton was surprised by all the commotion and looked totally confused. But he was already picking up. "Just think of it Ricky", Peter said to me "just picture it, Buckingham Palace, big bearskin hat, hundreds of tourist birds clinging on your arm and taking pictures"

"Buckingham Palace?" Repeated Riverton.

We ignored him. "Yeah" I replied to Peter "and all those ceremonial parades down the Pall Mall on a big white horse, riding behind with Royal Coach!"

"Royal Coach?" repeated Riverton, looking from me to Peter.

"I've heard" said Heath, "that these lucky Guardsmen have to fight the birds off, which they have a waiting list of dolly birds ready to dive into bed with them".

Jock had moved up to join in.

"No wonder those bloody Guardsman always looks so knackered".

"Dive in their Bed?" repeated Riverton looking decidedly more cheerful.

"Yeah" I said again, patting Riverton on the shoulder "You don't know how lucky you are mate!"

Come on mate!" said Peter to Riverton "Aren't you coming for a NAAFI break?"

"'Spose so" he declared.

Ten minutes later Riverton was bragging in the NAAFI to anyone who would listen about how he had decided to transfer to Guards Division! That evening Riverton drove us mad chatting on and on about the Guards Division. He had gone down to the Education Centre in the afternoon and picked up recruiting leaflets and information about the Guards Division.

"Do you know?" he asked us,

"How many weeks of the year we spend on Royal Duties?"

"No!" we asked "How many?"

"Thirteen weeks of the year we will be Guarding Buckingham Palace and other Royal Residences!" he told us.

"And we are taught equestrian discipline, when your given a horse its for life".

"Is it" we replied in unison.

"Yeah and . . . " Riverton had found a new love. He went on and on late into Tuesday evening driving us to distraction. Most had gone to bed by the time someone from the other end of the room called out "For Christ's sake Riverton, give us a rest!". Someone hurled a boot in Riverton's general direction and Peter got up and turned out the lights.

Wednesday dawned. The day I had to report to the Medical Officer. We adopted a cunning plan. At breakfast I literally gorged myself. Peter had had a word with the Chef. I was served a king size breakfast. Had two-pint pots of tea and even finished off the odd sausage and fried bread others had left on their plates. Normally, within half an hour of arriving back at our room, I would be off to the toilet for a five-minute sit down. Today I said to myself "no way! You're staying right where you are until after I've seen the Medical Officer".

I busied myself with everything I could to take my mind off the need to sit down. Eventually ten o'clock and NAAFI break arrived. Peter, Heaton, Jock and I sat at the same table. I managed to down a Steak and Kidney Pie, half a plate of chips and a pint of coke! Now I had to go to the Medical Centre and report to the Medical Officer there.

I was conscious of the urgent need for a pee on the way up to the Medical Centre but managed to take my mind off it during the walk up there. On arrival I reported to the Reception Desk and was told to take a seat. The minute I sat down my bladder began to complain again. It was five to eleven. I couldn't sit down for very long. I got up and moved around the Reception area reading everything on the Notice Boards even down to the name of the printers in small print at the bottom. It was close on ten past eleven and the urge to go and do something was becoming a pressing problem. I was beginning to get desperate when, at long last, I was called in to the Doctor.

Once inside the Doctor, who was a Lt-Colonel by rank, asked me to be seated. I sat down in front of his desk. He rambled on about how I was getting on and did I have any problems. His voice faded in the distance as I clenched my buttocks, with hands on lap; I squeezed my bits and began to knock my knees together to stave of the inevitable.

After what seemed like an age he said, "Well lad, boots off, up on the scales, lets have a look at your weight". "Boots off!" My mind screamed at me. The boots laced up way above the ankle with leather bootlaces and seemed to take an age to get undone. If I could have got my hands on a pair of scissors I would have cut the damn things off. Scooping off the second boot I made a mad scramble for the scales. The Doctor 'ummed' and 'ahhhed' as he set the weights then finally said, "Well done my boy, you are seven stone ten, you really have put on some weight".

"Thank you, Sir" I told him.

"You are still under the required weight for you height, I will need to see you again next week".

"For Christ's Sake" I screamed at him in my mind, "get a move on! Get on with it!"

He sat writing something on my records for a moment or two. "Ok my lad, off you go".

I grabbed my boots and literally ran from his office. Once in the Reception I looked frantically around for the toilets. Ah a sign. There was an arrow pointing towards a set of double doors leading into a long corridor. I ran, smashed open the doors and ran headlong down the corridor.

How come is it? that whenever a man needs the toilet in a hurry, the first toilet he finds is always the ladies. I rushed on further down the corridor and in my haste almost ran past a door marked 'Gentlemen'. I frantically pushed the door open undoing my belt and the top button of my trousers as I went. Once inside I dived into the first cubicle I came to urgently pushing down my trousers as I went! "Ahhhhhh!" I sighed aloud "Thank God, such relief"

I must have sat there for a good ten minutes before finally, feeling refreshed and relieved, I got up and left. I got a strange look from the nurse in Reception as I walked by. "Thank you" I told her. On the way back I took a slight detour and dropped a penny in the scales in the NAAFI toilets. I was seven stone six. I had lost just over four pounds since leaving the Doctors office!

Back at Spider 10 Riverton was in the final stages of packing his kit. He had had time to reflect and was not looking as happy as he had just a few hours ago. A man entered the room. "Riverton!" he called out. "There is a Landrover parked out front for you".
We followed young Riverton out to the front of the Spider, some of us helping with his case, kit bag and other kit. Sgt Steel was out the front too.
"Good Luck!" he told Riverton shaking his hand, "I'm sure this is for the best and that you are going to do really well in the Guards". Everyone in the room stood out on the steps at the front of the Spider.
"Good Luck mate" someone called.

"Say hello to Tin Lizzie" shouted another.

Riverton came forward and bending almost double put his arms around me and gave me a few pats on the back.

"You've been a good mate!" he told me shaking my hand, then straightening up told Peter the same. He went around shaking everyone's hand.

"Not got all day lad," the driver of the Landrover told him "Get a move on!"

Riverton chucked his case, kit bag and other kit into the back of the Landrover and moved around and opened the passenger door. Tears were streaming down his cheeks as he called "Be seeing you, if you can't be good, be careful.

The driver of the Landrover said, "Get in you big girls blouse, lets go", and Riverton climbed aboard. We watched him leave before we returned to our room. The now vacant bed halfway down the right hand side stood out like a sore thumb. No one spoke. Finally, after a long period of total silence Jock said "Oh Well, one down, nineteen to go!"

Chapter 9
ME, VOLUNTEER, NEVER!

On Thursday everyone was a little subdued after the departure of young Riverton. There was less of the banter and fooling around we normally enjoyed after a busy day. We had had a particular grueling afternoon with a three-mile speed march followed by an hour's introduction to the assault course. We had not been anywhere near the assault course so far and for many of us, if we never saw it again, it would be too soon. The main problem for me was trying to get over the six-foot wall. After trying unsuccessfully for a good half hour I was finally helped over it by a couple of the lads, one facing the wall and the other kneeling behind him, I literally climbed over them. Following the six-foot wall was the rope swing over a pit full of thick muddy water. Many of us didn't make the other side and suffered an undignified fall into the sludge. After an hour at the assault course we ran wearily back to Spider 10 most of us covered from head to toe in thick mud.

Having showered, Peter, Heaton and I were making ready to go to the cook house for our evening meal when Sgt Steel entered the room with, you would never guess who, our illustrious Provost Sgt. The thick bandages around his head I had seen him with last Saturday had been replaced with several band aid plasters. "Need a volunteer!" Sgt Steel announced in a loud voice, "for tonight's guard duty. "One of the guard has been injured and we need a replacement," the Provost Sgt informed us.

No one moved and the room was filled with a tense silence. You could have heard a pin drop.

"What about it Houghton?" the Sgt asked me "After all you owe him one!"

The Provost Sgt glared at me but said nothing. "It would be like putting my head in the lion's mouth" I thought to myself.

"Well?" Sgt Steel asked again.

"I got time to go for my dinner?" I asked.

"Won't need you until seven o'clock" the Provost Sgt informed me.

"My father told me never to volunteer for anything!" I told Sgt Steel.

"Your father was right" he replied "But?"

"But I suppose so" I said.

"Alright then" the Provost Sgt said, "see you at the Guard Room at seven, don't be late!"

As the two Sgts left, Peter said, "You're mad! You shouldn't have volunteered"

"Oh well", I replied "But now they owe me".

At seven o'clock I reported to the Guard Room as ordered and was tasked with polishing and buffing the floors and corridors for the first hour. The Provost Sgt had gone home and I had never met the Cpl left in charge. After finishing off the cleaning duties we sat around for an hour enjoying a steaming hot cup of strong tea. The corned beef and cheese and onion sandwiches duly arrived at about a quarter to nine and I made sure I got my fair share. I did not know any of my fellow guards and for some reason most of them treated me with some suspicion, an outsider not to be trusted.

My first stint on guard was to patrol the perimeter fence as I had done the Friday before. The time dragged by. Just as it had done previously, but eventually my two-hour stint came to an end. My next stint would be from one a.m. until three and so, after a second cup of hot brew; I got my head down and went to sleep. I was woken up at a quarter to one by one of the other guards. He hadn't brought me a cup of tea I noted. He just informed I had fifteen minutes before my next stag.

I got up and made myself a tea and also helped myself to one of the left over cheese and onion sandwiches, which were, by now, curling up at the edges.

"What's the score?" I asked the Cpl.

"As before" he told me, "the camp perimeter" and, with pickaxe handle in hand, off I went.

I reported back at half past one and again at two o'clock.

"Looks like I will get through this guard unscathed" I thought to myself as I once more started the long walk around the inside of the perimeter fence. I was as always bored to tears with patrolling the fence, kicking the end of my pickaxe handle with the toe of my boot, which I now did habitually. I never took any notice of what was going on outside the fence. There was just the road, the hedge and miles of fields. At about every 25 to 30 meters one of the fence uprights had a small light hanging on the outside. The lights were not very bright and were not much use. "A complete waste of electricity" I thought to myself.

However, at about two fifteen, I did notice something glitter in the darkness thanks to one of these rather dim lights. I bent down to see what it was, expecting to find a ring pull of a beer can or something, but it wasn't, it was a two shilling piece. As I bent to pick up the coin I noticed, just six inches or so further on, another coin, this time a half crown piece. A little further on there was a little group of coins, a couple of sixpences, a couple of shillings, several two-shilling pieces and half crown pieces.

"Someone must have a hole in their pocket," I thought to myself as I gathered up the coins. It was then I saw the brown paper bag. It was laying on its side a foot away one side split from about half way down to the bottom of the bag. From the hole in the bag there spilled a great pile of silver coins. All sixpences, shillings, two shilling and half crown pieces. I was rich! Gathering up all the coins I filled every available pocket that I had. Trouser side pockets, map pocket, breast pockets, shirt pockets, every pocket. I then screwed up the brown paper bag and threw it over the fence before making my way back to the Guard Room.

The situation reminded of a story my father once told me about his service in Korea. He was based at an Engineer Stores depot somewhere south of Seoul. It had been a terrible winter, he told me, and his squadron had seen no extra rations for Christmas. It was December 23rd and he and his mates had given up all hope of receiving any extra goodies. He and a couple of mates decided to raid the 'Yankee' base a couple of miles down the track.

So in the early hours of Christmas Eve morning, they blackened their faces and arms, and set out on a Commando style raid. He and his compatriots managed to secure several extra ten man ration packs, some extra cigarettes, and a crate or two of extra beer. Purely by chance my father came across a wooden cupboard in the US PX Club secured by a padlock. Ignoring the padlock and wrenching the cupboard open by removing the hasp itself he found a cash box, which he promptly liberated. Back in the British lines he forced open the cashbook to find about two thousand dollars worth of cash. They knew that before long, probably around breakfast time, the Yanks would discover their loss and a search would be instigated.

My father took the cash tin, before dawn, and counting the number of posts from the main gate, decided to bury the cash box at the twelfth post he came to. This he did. He and his compatriots agreed to wait for a week or two before recovering their loot. A few days later, my father woke up to a buzz of excitement. When he emerged from his pup tent discovered that a move was afoot. The whole Squadron was to be ready to move by first light the next morning to a point north of Seoul. He knew he would have to retrieve his cash box at the earliest opportunity. Unfortunately, when my father went out after dusk, shovel in hand, he found that the fencing had all been taken down. There were no posts. There was just a wide-open space, where previously, there had been a large barbed wire fence. Despite he and his mates spending half the night trying to recover their cash tin it could not be found.

Back to my sentry duty I could hear the coins jiggling about in my pockets as I walked. I wondered what to do? Do I report the find?

"Why the hell should I?" I argued with myself.

"Finders keepers that's what I say".

However by the time I got to the Guard Room I had convinced myself that the best thing to do was to report the find and hand in the cash. I walked up the steps jingling merrily away and entered the Guard Room. I had barely stepped one foot inside the guardroom when!

"You!" came an angry shout from an Officer I had never seen before.

"Don't you dare come walking in here while I am talking" he roared at me.

I stood stock-still.

"Now whoever broke into the NAAFI" the Officer continued "and stole the money from those vending machines will not get away with it!"

He took a moment or two to glare at me.

"Searches will be made of all living accommodation commencing shortly and what I want you all to do is to watch out for anyone who is suddenly well off!" He paused for a moment running his eyes along the rank of soldiers tasked with guarding the camp.

"Also keep your eyes open for anyone who possesses an unusual amount of silver coins" he said, and as if we didn't know what a silver coin was, went on, "that's sixpences, shillings, two shillings and half crowns, you all understand?"

There was a muted murmur of "Yes, Sir!" by the guard.

"I said do you understand?" he shouted.

"Yes, Sir" they all shouted back.

The Officer nodded to himself, then dismissed the men and strutting around me walked out of the Guard Room slamming the door behind him. I had not had the chance to speak.

"You!" the Cpl said, pointing at me, "You still have half an hour stag, so get moving!"

I got moving, and chink, jingle, chink, chinked my way back down the steps of the Guard Room and back on Patrol. As it happened Spider 10 was quite close to the perimeter fence and only a couple of hundred yards from the Guard Room. Without really thinking about it I found myself heading towards Spider 10. When I got there I went to my room, my bed was first on the left, and so tip toeing in I slid my case from under my bed. Taking great care not to make any noise I removed two pairs of socks from the case and tip toed back out.

Once outside I continued with my patrol. At the furthest point of my patrol, well away from the area I had found the coins, I took out the two pairs of socks and filled them with the coins from my pockets. I kept almost a pounds worth. I estimated that there must be about forty pounds worth of silver. I had enough money to last me to the end of my training, and then some. I searched around for a suitable hiding place and found a small culvert that ran under the perimeter fence to the ditch at the edge of the road. There I stashed my four socks and made my way back to the Guard Room.

The next morning the lads flooded me with questions about why the Spider had been searched and I told them the truth, the NAAFI had been broken into, all the vending machines raided and someone had got away with all the money. I even repeated to them the Officers warning to watch out for anyone who was flouting money about or who seemed to have an inordinate amount of silver coins. An added benefit was that both Sgt Steel and the Provost Sgt had been grateful for my volunteering for the Guard Duty and both considered me as a 'good egg''.

I resolved not to touch the money for at least a fortnight and did manage to resist the temptation. A fortnight later my first purchase was a watch, a Timex, not too expensive but good enough. I visited my little hoard whenever cash flow became tight. I never told a soul, not even Peter. Whenever I got the opportunity I changed small amounts into ten shilling or one pound notes and in this way managed to send my dad five pounds in return for giving the three pounds he had given to me when I left home. All in all life was looking quite rosy!

Chapter 10
ARMY HOCKEY FINALS

Late on Friday afternoon my fellow roommates and I were enjoying a period of 'make & mend'. Checking over our kit, cleaning, repairing little tears if we had to, and getting it all spick and span ready for the following Monday. Next week, we had been told, we would be going out on our first three day exercise during which we would be putting into practice our newfound map reading, weapon handling and camouflage training. We found the prospect of camping out for two nights rather exciting. It was like being allowed out to play cowboys and Indians and being paid for doing it.

I was making my way back from the toilets, a 'Commando' comic tucked under my arm when I saw someone walking down the corridor towards the troop office. He looked familiar but he had his back to me and I only got a glimpse of him as he turned the corner. I followed him and was just in time to see him turn into the Troop Office.

"It could not be!" I whispered out loud to myself "He is in Germany last I heard".

I walked up to the Notice Board next to the Troop Office. As usual the door was not fully closed.

""Hiya mate!" I heard the man say. It must be Jamie, my oldest brother, it sounds just like him. "What's he doing here?" I asked myself. I was a little worried by his sudden appearance.

"Well, well, look what the cats dragged in"? I heard Sgt Steel say, "How's it going Jamie?"

"Can't complain", I heard Jamie tell him.

"I heard you were a full screw" Sgt Steel exclaimed, "What happened?"

"Got busted for brawling with a couple of stroppy krauts!" Jamie declared.

"Don't you ever learn, Houghton? So what brings you here?"

"I'm in the Corps Hockey Team and we are in the final of the Army Championships in Aldershot on Sunday" Jamie replied.

"Yeah, So what brings you here?" Sgt Steel asked for a second time.

"Had a letter from my Mother" said Jamie.

"Oh how nice!" interjected Sgt Steel sarcastically.

"Yep, told me my little brother Ricky had been placed in your tender care!"

"You're not young Houghton's older brother? I should have guessed. Put two and two together!" said Steel.

"Well is he here?" asked Jamie "How is he doing?"

"Don't ask!" declared Sgt Steel and recounted all my deeds and misdeeds from day one.

Lt Mortimer and the windowlene, the beating up of the Provost Sgt, the breaking of a pool cue over the head of the hard case and, sadly, all about my poor physical fitness. Sgt Steel was a good storyteller and him and Jamie were having a really good laugh at my expense. He finished off by telling Jamie, "He's a good kid, trying very hard, so long as he keeps his nose clean and can improve his fitness, he'll pass out with everyone else". I was gratified to hear Sgt Steel tell Jamie this, even though I was eavesdropping.

Then Jamie asked "I know strictly speaking he isn't allowed off the camp yet but do you think I could take Ricky along to the Hockey match on Sunday afternoon?"

"I doubt it, they're a bit strict about the first four weeks as you know, but I'll check with the Squadron". I heard Sgt Steel pick up the phone and his side of the conversation with someone at the other end. Then the phone went down.

"The Sgt Major has reluctantly agreed, seeing as its you, but holds you personally responsible in ensuring he is back in camp by Dinner" Sgt Steel told Jamie.

"Great!" declared Jamie, "I'll go tell him. What room is he in?"

"One" replied Sgt Steel. I made a quick dash back down the corridor and into my room. I was sitting on my bed ostensibly bulling a pair of boots when Sgt Steel walked in.

"On you feet, Houghton!" he bellowed. I stood up; boot over one hand, yellow duster over the other. He crooked a finger at me saying, "Come with me". I put down the boot and duster and followed him out of the door.

There was Jamie. I did my best to act surprised to see him but really was pleased he'd come to see his little brother. I had never seen Jamie in army uniform before and he looked and acted the part very well. I felt a surge of pride for my big brother.

"'Ahm ya doin ah kid?" he asked me. He had unconsciously reverted to the Black Country twang.

"Fine", I told him "Wha' yow dewin' 'ere?" I asked, as if I didn't already know.

"Muth wrote 'n told me yowm 'ere" he said. "Thought I'd bet-ah pop in 'n see if yowm OK!"

"Ahm fine!" I told him again. Jamie then told me about the Army Hockey Championship finals on Sunday and asked if I would like to come along and watch. I didn't know a thing about hockey but the opportunity of getting off camp for a few hours, with my big brother to boot, was not to be missed.

"Would I ever!" I told him.

"Right then", he said "A coach will be leaving the Guardroom at ten thirty Sunday morning' with me an' me 'ockey team mates, I'll meet yow on tha coach".

"Okay!" I said.

"Great!" said Jamie "An dow yow be late!" With that he put out his hand, ruffled my hair and gave me a pat on the cheek. "See yow then ah kid!" and with that he turned, thanked Sgt Steel and left.

When I told my mates back in the room that my elder brother was playing in the Army Hockey Championship finals and that I was going to be allowed to go and watch on Sunday they were green with envy.

"You're a Jammy Sod!" Peter told me "You have the luck of the devil!"

"And I will make the most of it", I told Peter, "believe me, if there is a chance for a quick pint or two I'll grab it".

"Yeah, well", replied Peter, "If you do, have one for me, won't you?".

"You bet I will!" I responded enthusiastically, "or even two or three".

Needless to say that for the remainder of Friday and all of Saturday I had a perpetual grin on my face and my excitement grew by the hour. I paced about impatiently, wishing my life away.

"For God's sake!" Heath shouted at me, "go read a book or something, you are getting on my nerves pacing up and down!"

Sunday morning finally arrived and fearful of missing the coach I made my way down to the Guard Room before ten o'clock to wait it. I was wearing the clothes that Peter had given to me. The clothes which had once belonged to his fourteen year old little brother. I had never felt so smartly dressed. The coach was already there when I got there but there was no one about. Not even the driver, so I found myself pacing up and down impatiently for half an hour. At long last, just before ten thirty, I saw a group of men walking down the road toward the bus. They were dressed in white shorts and wearing the dark red and blue stripped shirts depicting the Corps colours. The Corps badge was also displayed on the rugby style shirts. They looked very impressive to me.

Jamie saw me before I saw him and from the midst of the group of men shouted

"Hiya Ricky, you made it then?"

"Yeah, course I did" I called back.

"Been waiting long?" he asked.

"Nah, just got here" I lied.

"Hey lads!" Jamie called out, "This is my little kid brother, Ricky, known locally as Wam Bam The Windowlene Man". They all laughed.

Of course, Jamie had to explain to them why?

I received a babble of greetings from the men as they filed passed and on to the coach. Jamie and I boarded last, Jamie took a seat next to one of his mates and I found myself having to sit at the front next to the driver. The coach moved off, down the road, and out of the main gate. I was out of camp for the first time in two weeks.

During the forty minute drive to Aldershot there was a lot of banter, cat calls and whistles at ladies as we drove through Farnborourgh, including graphic descriptions of their fate should any of them dare to accept the many invitations made by the team to board the coach. I had never heard such language before or indeed anything like those graphic descriptions. I was quite embarrassed when I heard Jamie joining in such coarse frivolity. He even called across to me and asked me whether or not I would kick a particularly top heavy young lady, who was waiting at the traffic lights to cross the road, out of my bed, which made me blush profusely.

During the later part of the journey they were considerably quieter and I could feel the nervousness and tension building as they contemplated the game ahead. They had last minute discussions on set moves and tactics almost all of which went completely over my head. I had never seen a hockey match before and to be quite honest, until Jamie had me asked to go and watch this one, had believed hockey was a ladies game. Though I dared not say so in front of this lot! They would have thrown me of the coach in two seconds flat.

"Almost there!" I heard the driver say as we approached another Army Barracks and the men started to pull hold alls and other equipment from the racks above their heads in readiness for disembarking from the bus.

Once off the bus Jamie and the team moved off to the large changing rooms off to one side and to put on their boots and shin pads. Jamie directed me to stand on the other side of the pitch and told me to watch the game from there.

"Once the game is over", he told me "come over to the dressing rooms and wait for me there". I walked over to the stand I thought Jamie had indicated which had the word 'vips' in block letters at the foot of the steps.

"What are 'vips' I wondered as I climbed up and took a front row seat at the centre of the stand? Several people, some in full dress uniform, arrived a little later to take their seats. Some gave me a curious look as they filed onto the stand but said nothing.

Then I heard a band playing and the Royal Engineer Band marched out from behind the changing rooms and out onto the field. They played some excellent music which was really inspiring and again I felt a surge of pride for my brother Jamie taking part in such a stirring event. In front of me, just in front of the stand, there was a small stage with white ropes to the front and sides. Several Officers in full dress uniforms, complete with swords and what appeared to be a Mayor mounted this stand.

The band marched forward playing 'Wings', the Corps March, before coming to a halt in front of the stand. The Band Leader and one of the Officers exchanged words, I couldn't hear what was being said, then they saluted each other before the Band Leader turned and marched back to his Band. They then played on during a last circuit of the hockey field. As the band marched off the two teams ran from the dressing rooms onto the pitch to a thunderous roar of shouts and applause from the crowds surrounding the pitch. Within minutes they bullied off and the game was under way.

Once the game was under way a dozen or so soldiers in best No. 1 Dress Uniforms began moving around my stand handing out little bits of pastry with prawns or tuna stuffed inside and little salmon and cucumber sandwiches, cheese biscuits and all manor of nice titbits. Others circulated with glasses of champagne, red and white wine and glasses of orange juice. As I looked around the perimeter of the hockey field and the large crowd around it slowly began to dawn on me that perhaps I was not in the right place!

I noticed a Beer Tent behind one of the goals from which most of the crowds were heading to get there own drinks. Here I was being waited on hand and foot and drinking, I imagined, someone's expensive champagne. I looked to the left and right along the row in which I was seated. It was full of Officers and their ladies. I thought if I tried to leave now it would draw attention to myself so decided, unless told otherwise, to stay put.

However it was not long, about ten minutes into the game, before Jamie scored the first goal for our team. I was on my feet in an instant and climbing onto my seat screamed hysterically, "Jamie! Jamie! Yahoo!" Punching the air with my fists in time with the shouts. I don't know if Jamie heard me or not but he waved his hockey stick in salute to those on the stand. When I looked around I saw that practically everyone on the stand were watching me and not the game! I sat down looking and feeling rather sheepish. Nevertheless a third glass of champagne was being offered so I took it and raised my glass to those around me who were still staring in my direction.

I was beginning to feel a little flushed from the three glasses of champagne and so I refused the fourth, taking a large glass of red wine and a slack handful of the tit-bits instead. Shortly before half time the Royal Engineers scored again. I nearly choked on one of those little salmon and cucumber sandwiches, which was just as well because as we scored all eyes turned to me to watch my reaction.

By the time we scored the third, half way through the second half and my second glass of red wine, I was beginning to feel a little sloshed. I vowed to myself that I would not have another. "I've had enough"! I told myself several times. However the temptation was to great and could not resist a third glass of wine as tray floated by. I sat sipping it daintily until full time. After a really exciting last twenty minutes and a flurry of goals the final score was 6 - 4 to us.

I wished I had had a camera as Jamie and the rest of the team did a circuit of the hockey field holding a magnificently large silver cup aloft. As Jamie ran past my stand clutching one handle of the cup he looked very surprised to see where I was sitting. He raised on of his arms as if to say "What the hell you doing there?" I shrugged.

The game over, people were leaving the stand from either side. I rose, on slightly wobbly legs, to go to the Changing Rooms to find Jamie. "'Scuse me, Sir!" I said attempting moving past a rather paunchy Officer. He turned and looking me up and down asked "Just to satisfy my curiosity my boy, but who are you?"

"I'm Houghton, Sir," I told him.

"From?" he asked.

"From Friar Park, Wednesbury" I told him.

"Who are you with?" He sighed at me.

"I'm with my brother, he scored the first goal," I said happily.

"You have an invitation for the VIP stand?" he asked. "An invitation?" I replied.

"Yes, you have to have an invitation to sit in the VIP stand and to attend the reception after the game" he told me holding up a white card with pretty writing on it and gold trim around the edges.

"No, Sir" I replied, "I didn't know I needed one!"

"Well my boy" he asked "Answer me this, do you intend joining us at the reception too?"

"No, Sir" I told him "I'm going to meet my brother at the changing rooms".

"Thank goodness for that!" said the Officer with a grin and lead the way off the stand.

I hadn't got long to wait at the changing rooms before Jamie and the team emerged and made their way back to the coach. In no time we were on our way back to Cove. As if by magic, bottles of beer were appearing from every corner of the coach. Jamie sat next to me for the return trip.

"What on earth were you doing on VIP stand?" he asked me.

"I thought that's were you told me to sit" I replied.

"No! I said to go stand on the other side!" He told me "Not sit on the stand"

"What's VIP then?" I asked.

"The VIP stand is for Very Important Persons", Jamie said "Like the Chief Royal Engineer, who is a General, and all the Brigadiers and Colonels and their ladies".

"Well how was I to know?" I said.

"Didn't anyone say anything?" Jamie asked.

"No, they just kept giving me champagne, wine and titbits and the occasional funny look!"

"Hey lads!" Jamie shouted, "Rickey was only centre stage in the VIP stand being waited on hand and foot".

"Yeah" someone shouted, "I thought it was him, standing on his seat and screaming like a lunatic".

Everyone laughed at this. Shortly after they began singing rude rugby songs Jamie kneeling on his seat facing back into the bus conducting everyone with his two hands. I didn't know any of the songs but with a bottle of freshly opened M&B's in my hand, made a fair to middling attempt at joining in.

I don't want to join the Army
I don't want to go to war
I'd rather 'ang around Piccadilly Underground
Living off the earnings of a high borne lady
Don't want a bayonet up me arsehole
Don't want me bollocks blown away
I'd rather stay in England
Merry, Merry England
And fornicate the stupid life away

..... Cor blimey

Monday, I touched her on the ankle
Tuesday I touched her on the knee
Wednesday success, I lifted up her dress
Thursday she said Oh Cor Blimey
Friday I put me 'and upon it
Saturday she gave me such a squeeze
And Sunday after Super
I wopped the bugger upper
And now I'm paying thirty bob a week

. . . . . Cor Blimey

Also included in their repertoire were such favourites as 'Sweet Chariot' and 'Old MacDonald had a Farm'. The verses about the 'Ram' and 'Turkey' in 'Old MacDonald had a Farm' just happened to coincide with our arrival in, and slow progress through, Farnborough town centre. If there was anyone not close enough to hear us on the coach, they could certainly understand what we were singing about, as almost everyone on the bus, including myself, were going through all the actions required in the song.

All too soon we arrived back at Southwood Camp, Cove and turned into the main gate. "Now" said Jamie "Go back to your room, have a chat with your mates, report to the troop office that you're back on time OK".

"Ok" I replied.

"Meet me back here at seven o'clock" he ordered

"Why?" I asked.

"You don't have to if you don't want to" he said, "but if you want a last quick drink with your big brother, meet me at seven".

"When are you going back to Germany?" I asked him

"Early Tuesday morning" he replied.

"Ok, I'll be here" I told him and walked quickly back to Spider 10.

Back in my room I related the game, the score, and the fact that I'd sat in a VIP stand throughout to my mates. Some believed me, about the champagne and wine, but I think most of them did not, believing I was trying to pull a fast one.

"Coming to Dinner?" Peter asked me.

"No, I'm still chocka from all those little sandwiches and stuff and the champagne" I told him.

"First time I've known you to miss out on your dinner" Heath told me.

"Told you, I'm still chocka, besides I'm meeting me brother shortly and we are going for a last drink before he goes back to Germany"

"Where you going?" Peter asked.

"To the NAAFI I suppose, where else can we go?" Off I went.

When I arrived back at the Guard Room at five to seven there was a Ford Cortina parked where the coach had parked earlier. Jamie hung his head out of the passenger window. "Come on, chop! Chop!" he called "Jump in the back".

"Where we going?" I asked. "We'll know when we get there!" said Jamie.

"But I was told to make sure I was back in camp by six!" I explained

"You were back in camp by six weren't you?" Jamie asked.

"Yeah but!" I replied hesitantly.

"Just get in," said Jamie "or my mates might think you're just a big girls blouse!"

I got in and we were moving as I slammed the door. We went out through the main gate and pulled up at the road. "Which way?" asked the driver.

Jamie tossed a coin. "Right!" He declared. The driver put his foot down did a tyre screeching turn to the right and roared off into the sunset.

Half an hour later we arrived at a large country pub, which appeared to be in the middle of nowhere. However when we went in the pub was packed out. Most sitting around tables crammed with empty and half full glasses of beer, cigarette ashtrays overflowing onto the tables. A few were playing darts and I could hear the distinctive clack of pool balls being knocked around the table in the next room. Jamie led us to the corner of the bar to a recently vacated table and the four of us sat around it. Jamie introduced me to his friends.

"This is Sandie" he introduced; Sandie leaned across the table and shook my hand.

"And this is Doug" said Jamie. I turned slightly to shake Doug's hand.

"We've met!" said Doug giving my hand a brief shake. I almost fell of my chair with shock and surprise.

I was speechless. I didn't recognize him out of uniform and without his beret. He looked totally different. Doug was none other than the infamous Sgt Steel. Jamie moved off to the very crowded bar.

"Me and Jamie go way back" explained Doug "We were in training together!"

Finding my voice I asked, "How come you're a Sgt and Jamie isn't?"

"I haven't been caught", laughed Doug. "And I don't want to be caught".

"Oh" I said not knowing what else to say.

"So" Doug went on "You are not here, and I am not here, savvy?"

"Savvy!" I confirmed. Jamie turned up with two pints of beer each, "to save queuing again", he explained.

Fancy a game of pool. Jamie and Doug had the first game on the pool table and naturally the story of my incident at the pool table in the NAAFI the previous week arose and I had to re-tell the story of what had happened for the benefit of Jamie and Sandie. By half past nine I knew that I was going to have one hell of a hangover the next day. We had moved from pool to darts. They told Doug about how I had gate crashed the VIP stand that afternoon.

"Typical", he exclaimed, "Can't take you Houghton's anywhere!"

This reminded me of my earlier consumption that explained the sickly feeling of champagne, wine and beer sloshing around in my stomach. I was learning though.

"Am dying for a crap" I told Jamie as I pushed my chair back, "all those sandwiches and things". I did not go to the nearest toilets but moved through the pub to toilets on the other side. Finding that had regular customers I went out of the side door of the pub and moved around the side where I found a row of bins partly hidden by a clump of bushes. There I was violently sick for the second time in my life.

When I eventually returned to the table Jamie asked what had taken me so long. I told him that some one had made a mess in the nearest toilets hence when I got to the other toilet there was a bit of a queue. I am sure that my eyes were a little bloodshot but they all seemed to accept my story without question. However by eleven o'clock, when the pub closed I was practically legless, falling over a stool on the way out and being virtually carried by non-other than Sgt Steel. I do not remember the journey back to camp or my walk back to Spider 10 and my room.

The first I remember was being woken five thirty as normal by the room Cpl. "Up Houghton" he shouted. I forced open my blearing eyes, putting my hand immediately to my head at the sudden pain. My head was throbbing. The Cpl ordered me to report to the Troop Office immediately. It seemed to take an age to get dressed hopping on one leg to get my trousers on and falling back onto my bed.

"Come on" bellowed the Cpl "I haven't got all day".

I struggled into my boots, laced them as best I could and headed for the door buttoning up the last few buttons of my shirt as I went.

At the Troop Office I was met by a rather bleary eyed Sgt Steel who seemed to be trying very hard to look his best but in so doing looking quite terrible.

I stood to attention in front of the desk.

"You wanted to see me Sgt?"

"Yes, Houghton" he said loudly, and then grimaced "I heard you are a bit under the weather?"

"Am a bit Sgt," I confirmed

"There seems to be a bit of bug going around I'm told," he said "you best be confined to your room till lunchtime, don't want you passing it around!"

"Yes, Sgt" I replied

"Dismiss" he said with a wave of his hand. Mischievously, I came, very loudly, to attention, did a smart about turn, slamming my right foot down in a smart soldierly manner, and marched noisily from the office. As I left the Troop Office my Room Cpl walked in. I paused to listen for a minute to see if Sgt Steel would reveal to the Cpl what went on the previous night.

"I'm taking the morning off" I heard him say "See you after lunch".

I turned and made my way gratefully back to bed.

I never did meet up with Jamie again while he was serving in the Army. We always appeared to be in separate countries, and quite often, not even on the same continent. He loved his sports. He also played Football. Rugby, Ice Hockey at a high level. He also took every opportunity to go skiing, sailing or anything that happened to be on offer.

I heard that prior to the following years Army Hockey Champion-ships Jamie badly broke his right leg playing polo and was in plaster for months. He never did play any sport competitively after that and I knew when I heard that it was the beginning of the end of Jamie's military career. Never having been really interested in climbing the ladder Jamie left the army a couple of years later and settled down with his new girlfriend Jane.

Chapter 11
THE BIG SEARCH

Monday arrived and after the morning PT we spent most of the remainder of the day preparing for the three-day exercise that would be starting on Tuesday morning. We drew our 24 hour ration packs, one-man pup tents, sleeping bags and all manor of equipment that would be needed over the next three days. We packed our large packs with spare clothing, our rations, and some extra goodies we bought from the NAAFI, such as extra chocolates, biscuits and sweets. Every hour we would wear our large packs and full fighting order to test the weight. We would jump up and down and jiggle about to make sure nothing rattled. The first time I put on my own large pack I immediately fell backwards onto my bed. "God almighty!" I exclaimed, "How the hell do they expect me to carry this!" In our kidney pouches went our Mess Tins with our brew kit in one and washing and shaving kit in the other. It was very late Monday night before we were satisfied that we had everything we needed and crawled into bed. I went out like a light; it had been a long day.

On Tuesday we loaded all our large packs onto a three ton truck. We then went to draw our rifles and thirty-six rounds of blank ammunition. I was surprised when Sgt Steel ordered me to draw a Bren Gun, A light machine gun, and he ordered Heaton to be my number two. The number two carried extra ammunition for the Bren and also the cleaning and repair kit, which included a spare barrel.

When using the Bren Gun the number two would feed me with ammunition as I needed it. He would also assist in changing the barrel if the barrel overheated. We were all also issued with a thunder flash each. A thunder flash, which was like a large firework, was what we used instead of hand grenades and we received a demonstration of their power before we left. One of the Cpls struck a thunder flash, placed it under a tin hat, and made a hasty retreat. When the thunder flash exploded it threw the tin hat some thirty feet or more in the air!

At half past eight and still feeling bloated from breakfast we all climbed aboard the three ton truck and we were off. There was a babble of excited chatter as we drove off into the countryside. We were all looking forward to the next three days with a mixture of fear and excitement. I hoped that I would not be expected to lug the Bren Gun around for the whole of the three days. I had been prone, during my first two weeks, of putting things down and forgetting where I'd left them and had been bawled out on more than one occasion by Sgt

Steel or the Cpl for not being able to put my hand to a particular piece of kit when asked to. "I really must be careful" I thought to myself "that during this exercise I keep tabs on all my kit!"

We drove for over an hour to Salisbury Plain and were finally dropped of in a sparsely wooded area in the middle of nowhere. We spent the next hour and a half being taught how to camouflage our tin hats, back packs and equipment and how to move quietly through the woods.

We were then allowed an hour to make a brew and enjoy a snack before moving out. We were split into two sections, one of ten and one of nine, and with ten to fifteen yards between each man we set out on our first march of the day.

To my surprise I didn't find lugging my large pack and Bren Gun quite as hard as I had expected and I was not the first to start to lag behind. After two hours on the march we were told to halt and take up defensive positions, to 'Stand To'. The Cpl walked around the area giving each man his arc of fire and a warning to keep our ears and eyes open. We lay in our defensive positions until just after two o'clock whereupon we were instructed to 'Stand Down' and make our own lunches.

We ripped open our large packs and pulled out our hexamine burners and within no time at all we were boiling up stew and dumplings in one mess tin and spotted dick and custard in the other. No sooner than the majority of us had finished cooking and about to tuck in when we heard a rifle shot followed almost immediately by the thunderous crack of a thunder flash! There was a mad scramble for our rifles and fighting order, many of us running around like headless chickens, the excitement just too much to bear.

"Stand To! Stand To" the Cpls screamed at us and we all made a scramble back to our defensive positions. "Bren Gunner over here!" I heard Sgt Steel call and Heaton and I made a dash in the general direction of the voice.

"Here" shouted Sgt Steel "Set up your Bren here and cover the track ahead and twenty five degrees either side". Heaton and I could hear one or two of the lads firing their rifles and wondered what or whom they were firing at.

There was another load bang, much closer this time, as a thunder flash landed within our defensive circle. I was out of breath from running with the Bren Gun and with the excitement of my first 'action'. Within minutes a land rover came into view and with his foot down, the driver came charging down the track towards us. I could tell it was the enemy by the red flag flying from its aerial.

I took aim with the Bren Gun, flicked off the safety catch, and pressed the trigger. There was a dull click. In all the excitement, had forgotten to load the damn thing!

"Magazine!" I screamed into Heaton's left ear, forgetting that I had two full magazines of my own. Heaton pulled a magazine from his right pouch and thrust it into my hand. I flicked open the magazine cover and pushed it home.

"What the blazes are you doing Houghton?" screamed Sgt Steel "Waiting to see the whites of their eyes?"

The Landrover was practically on top of us before I finally got to let go with a long burst from the Bren Gun. The Landrover careered off the track in a rather convincing mock crash between two trees.

"Bet they've practiced that a few times!" I thought to myself.

As quickly as they had appeared the enemy vanished back into the woods and we had nothing to do but keep our defensive position in place for half an hour or so until we were sure they had gone. Then came the word to "Stand Down". We made our way back into our encampment; some to find their lunch stone cold, and for those who had not had the foresight to remove the food from the hexamine burners, burnt to a frazzle. Having eaten our lunches, brewed a tin of tea we repacked our large packs and cleared up the area to make sure no litter was left to give away our position. Towards four o'clock we were again on the move.

We were attacked twice more during the afternoon and I was thoroughly enjoying myself. With the adrenalin pumping through my veins I had forgotten about the weight I was carrying and my aching arms from lugging the Bren Gun over I don't know how many miles. As the light began to fade we arrived at another wooded area. It could have been the same one for all I knew and the Training Cpl's could have just marched us in a big circle! However, after going through the now familiar 'Stand To' routine we were told to erect our pup tents and prepare to camp for the night.

We had to camouflage our tents and the Cpl gave us a hard time until he was satisfied that they could not be seen from any distance. I was particularly pleased that the Cpl had been satisfied with my attempt at his first visit. I'd obviously done a reasonable job of camouflaging my tent.

A guard roster was given verbally; I was on sentry duty from eleven p.m. until one a.m. We had to make sure we knew where the next on duty's pup tent was so you didn't disturb others unnecessarily. We were far quicker preparing and eating our evening meal than we were at lunchtime fearing that we would be again attacked and the food ruined. It was now getting very dark and with the exception of the two on sentry duty we were all told to get our heads down. No sooner had I dropped off to sleep when, you guessed it, we had yet another 'Stand To'. I must confess that seeing the muzzle flashes from my Bren Gun in the darkness were very impressive and I felt like John Wayne fighting two German Panzer Divisions single handed. A vision came to mind of me standing on a small hillock, ammunition belts across my chest, firing the Bren Gun from the hip. Hundreds of Germans or Japanese or whoever our favourite enemy was on the day, falling all around me.

All too soon I was awoken, yet again, this time for my stint of sentry duty. The only incident during the two hour stint was me falling over someone's pup tent in the dark and being cursed profusely for doing so. I did receive a minor injury. About half way through my stint I decided to take a leak and attempted, as you do, to approach a convenient tree. All I succeeded in doing was getting a bad poke in the eye from a hanging twig. I backed off from the tree and decided to relieve myself in the open, taking care that there was not some body's pup tent in the line of fire.

About ten minutes before my stint ended I went to wake Peter who just happened to be next. When he got up to relieve me I moved off to the area where I thought my tent was. Everything looked so different in the dark. I spent the next half an hour trying to find my tent, waking two or three of my mates in the process. In the end Peter suggested I use his until it gets light and I did so gratefully. Next morning the reason why I had failed to find my tent became clear. It had collapsed under the weight of my over enthusiastic camouflaging.

Wednesday carried on in much the same vein as the day before and by mid afternoon we were becoming quite proficient at moving tactically around the countryside and reacting well to any attack. That morning I had a word with Heaton, my number two, about taking turns in carrying the Bren Gun. My shoulders were not only rubbed raw by my large pack it was also being aggravated by the Bren Gun's strap. I had to show him my raw shoulder during a brief stop mid morning in order to convince him. He, very reluctantly, agreed. So for the rest of the day we would swap over our weapons every time we stopped.

Lt Mortimer joined us for lunch that day and had a little conflab with Sgt Steel. It was obvious that until now he had been acting as the enemy and that for the next few hours at least he had changed sides. At about three in the afternoon, while patrolling through a particularly wooded area, once again we were fired upon by our Training Team.

Heaton and I were now acting in a well-coordinated fashion and within a minute we were in position and blasting away at anything that moved. The fire fight went on for about twenty minutes. Then suddenly Lt Mortimer jumped to his feet, drew his pistol, and screamed, "Come on men! Charge! I'm right behind you!" A Freudian slip if ever there was one. We all scrambled to our feet and charged out of the woods and up a hill where we saw several men beating a hasty retreat. Having taken the hill and thoroughly routed the enemy we again formed up and moved out, Lt Mortimer taking the lead.

We marched around the countryside for two hours. Two or three of the lads began to flag again. Not me, I'm John Wayne! Visions of me leading a rough group of leathernecks behind enemy lines came to mind. My imagination was running amok. "The hell I will!" I thought to myself in a broad American accent. At last, we approached another wooded area, or the same one again, I couldn't tell which.

Lt Mortimer decided to call a halt. "Bren Gunner" he shouted. Heaton and I trotted across to him. Indicating a ditch at the side of the road he said, "Take up your position here, arc of fire from that fallen tree, across the track, to there!" he told us sweeping his arm from left to right. We both jumped into the ditch. I looked at Heaton, Heaton looked at me. We both said together,
"The Bren Gun! You've left the Bren Gun behind".
"I didn't, you did!" we both said again.
"You were carrying it last" I told Heaton

"Yeah, but then it should have been your turn!" he responded.

"It was not a proper stop, you should have grabbed the Bren when we charged up the hill" I told Heaton.

"I had the cleaning kit," he yelled at me. There followed a five minute argument in a hushed whisper each of us blaming each other for leaving the Bren Gun behind. Heaton sealed my fate by saying. "Well its your personal weapon, you signed for it, it was your responsibility!" I climbed out of the trench and approached the Lt and Sgt Steel who were standing off to one side sipping hot tea from a flask.

"'Scuse me, Sir" I interrupted.

"What is it Houghton?" the Lt asked.

I was so nervous I began to pat my jacket breast and trouser pockets with the palms of my hands, as if I was searching for something.

"I seem to have lost my Bren Gun," I stammered.

"You what!" screamed the Lt "What do you mean you've lost your Bren Gun?"

"How the hell can you lose a whopping great Bren Gun?" Sgt Steel shouted.

Everyone had stopped what they were doing and staring at the three of us.

"Me and Heaton were taking turns carrying it" I explained, "And when the Lt shouted charge, we charged! We forgot to pick up the Bren Gun!"

The Lt was red with rage. It was becoming apparent that he was close to panic!

"What are we going to do? I might have known you would do something like this, Houghton!" his voice rising by several octaves "What are we going to do?"

"Ok Sir" said Sgt Steel, "lets not panic, we haven't come that far we'll all go back and look for it".

"Yes, we'll fan out and look for it!" said Lt Mortimer "We'll find it!"

He did not sound very confident. I wasn't convinced we would either.

"Houghton" sighed Sgt Steel "how the hell can you forget something as big as a Bren Gun, it reaches from your head to your toes! It's bloody massive! I sure hope we find it!"

We trudged back the way we had come and when we arrived at the hill we thought we had charged up a few hours later we fanned out and did a sweep down and through the woods. We searched the woods thoroughly for the remainder of the day without success.

When it began to get dark Lt Mortimer, looking quite pale, said he would have to return to camp to report the loss. It was obvious to all of us that this was the end of the exercise. We camped where we were that night and the next morning resumed the search. We searched throughout all day Thursday to no avail. The Bren Gun was never found. It had simply disappeared.

We returned to camp Thursday night, handed in our rifles, sleeping bags and tents etc; and returned to our room to unpack and clean our kit. There was a strange silence. I was noticeably quite worried. My roommates worried about me.

"Hah!" Peter told me "What can they do?"

"They could chuck me out!" I replied.

"They won't do that" Heaton assured me, "It wasn't all your fault".

"This will be the last straw" I croaked, "they're bound to throw the book at me!"

"Well look on the bright side Ricky" said Jock from his bed. "They can't put you up against the wall and have you shot, times have changed!"

"Thanks" I moaned, "Think I'd rather be shot than chucked out!"

The next morning, Friday, I was once again banging the boards in front of the same Major who had fined me two shillings for clobbering the Provost Sgt, was it just a week ago? Lt Mortimer, Sgt Steel and poor young Heaton were all called to give evidence. It was a foregone conclusion that I would be found guilty of negligence. The Major summed up by saying that he could not understand how it was that I had marched around for some two hours without anyone, Lt Mortimer, Sgt Steel, any of the Training Cpls or anyone else noticing that I was not carrying my Bren Gun. However, I was to be held ultimately responsible for its safekeeping. Having asked me for the second time in my short military career if I would accept his punishment or elect trial by Courts Martial the Major fined me Two Shillings and Sixpence and I was put under stoppages off pay of Ten Shillings towards the cost of the Bren Gun.

That same Friday afternoon I was summoned before a Court of Inquiry into the loss of the Bren Gun. This time the Lt and Sgt Steel were called as witnesses along with one or two of the training NCOs.

At the head of the table was a Lt-Colonel and two Majors, one of which was the one that had fined me the ten shillings a couple of hours earlier. The questioning went on for a good hour. Each time our replies were being recorded diligently by each of them. They questioned Lt Mortimer about the routes we had taken and had we covered the routes properly during the search for the Bren Gun. He was asked, how come was it that a weapons check had not been carried out before leaving each location.

"I assumed that Sgt Steel had delegated weapon checks to the Training Cpls" he replied.

"Assumed?" queried the Lt-Colonel.

"Yes, Sir!" replied the Lt.

I was beginning to feel very sorry for Lt Mortimer.

"And you Sgt Steel, did you assume the Cpls would delegate themselves?"

I was feeling sorry for Sgt Steel too!

"No, Sir" replied Sgt Steel. The Court of Inquiry continued in this vein, both the Lt and Sgt Steel being questioned the most. They both were looking hot under the collar and very uncomfortable.

At one point I even imagined I saw the Lt's bottom lip quivering ever so slightly.

"And you, Houghton, you keep referring to that particular bush in which you had taken up your firing position, as the position the Bren Gun was left".

"Yes, Sir" I said in a hushed voice.

"How can you be sure Houghton, that that is where the Bren Gun was left? Could you have left it somewhere earlier?

"No, Sir" I replied "I remember thinking, as I was firing, by the hell I mustn't lose this or I'll be right in the shit!"

The three officers who had been very straight laced throughout the whole proceedings thus far suddenly found it extremely difficult to keep a straight face. The Major who had fined me the ten shillings had to cough in hand to control himself.

"Well, Gentlemen" said the Lt-Colonel "I think we have heard enough don't you?" They rose, gathering up all their papers, and filed out of the room. I was thinking about the week ahead. Would I still be here? Week four was to be our final week in what they called "Basic Military Training" and we would spend the best part of the week actually firing live ammunition on the ranges. We had to qualify in Stirling Sub Machine Gun, The Bren Gun, and the new 7.62 Self Loading Rifle. I hoped they wouldn't chuck me out or put me in jail before I had had a chance to fire real live bullets.

Both Lt Mortimer and Sgt Steel glared at me and then without a word they too filed out of the room leaving me standing all alone wondering what on earth I should do now? I went for my dinner!

Several years later, while serving in Germany, I received a credit in my pay. I looked at the paymaster.

"What is this for?" I asked him.

"A miscellaneous credit" he informed me.

"But what for?" I asked.

He looked at his notes, scratched his head, and said,

"Seems you were placed under stoppages of pay for something while you were in training, seems that they have now found it!"

Chapter 12
FINAL WEEK OF BASIC

The weekend passed quietly with little to do but prepare for three days of ranges from Monday to Wednesday. We were excited by the fact that this was our final week of basic. Those over eighteen years of age would be allowed out on Fridays and Saturdays until 10 p.m. The pubs closed at 11 p.m. Those unfortunate enough to still be under eighteen were only allowed out on Saturday and had to be back in camp by 7 p.m. We were told this was to prevent under age drinking. As if I would!

Early on Monday morning, straight after our breakfast, we had to draw our 7.62 SLR's and boarding a three ton truck drive out to the ranges about five miles from the camp. In order to complete our 'Basic Training' each of us had to classify in firing the SLR, the Bren and the SMG. Monday was dedicated to the SLR. Having arrived on the range each man was required to zero his rifles. This meant firing five rounds at a target form 100 yards. By inspecting where the rounds hit, the foresight and rear sights of the rifle could be adjusted to bring the aim centre target. When I fired my first five rounds they formed a grouping of about four inches between the centre and the left shoulder. Sgt Steel adjusted each person's rifle according to the hits on their targets.

"You have a good grouping there," he told me as he took my rifle from me. He adjusted my foresight a couple of turns and my rear sight half a turn.

I fired a second load of five rounds. I again achieved a tight grouping slightly left of centre.

"Very good, Houghton, very good". He gave my rear sight another tweak. Once Sgt Steel was happy that everyone's weapon was zeroed correctly we all moved back to the two hundred yard firing point.

At two hundred yards we were all issued with eighteen rounds each. There were to be five, six second, exposures of the target. We had to fire three rounds at each exposure.

"Prone position, down!" shouted Sgt Steel. We dropped to the ground. I was in lane four.

"With a magazine of eighteen rounds. Load!" he bellowed. We pulled out our magazines from our ammunition pouches and rammed them home.

"Watch and Shoot!" he called. A few seconds later up popped the target. I lifted the barrel, took aim, held my breath and fired the first round. Allowing the barrel to drop slightly, I lifted it up again, aimed, held my breath, and fired the second round. By the time I was about to take my third shot it seemed that everyone else had fired their three rounds straight off. Bam! Bam! Bam! I fired my third shot and half a second later the target dropped.   Five seconds later up they came again.

I repeated my firing as before, taking my time, holding my breath, unhurried, and firing. Within five minutes the first shoot was over. "Safety catches on," bellowed Sgt Steel "Stand Up!" "For inspection Port Arms" He went on. We cocked or rifles and removed our magazines placing them on top of the rifle.

In this way Sgt Steel could walk along the line and check that the magazines were empty and that there were no rounds left in the chamber. Having checked our rifles Sgt Steel picked up the radio and called for the scores.   Sixty percent was needed for a pass, eighty percent was Marksman. "Lane One?" he asked. "Forty-five".

"Lane Two?" "Sixty-Seven".

"Lane Three?"   This was my best mate Peter. "Eighty-Seven".

"Well done Duncan-Forbes" muttered Sgt Steel.

"Lane Four?" he went on.   "Maximum" came the response. "Say again Lane Four?" asked Sgt Steel. "Maximum 100" came the response. Sgt Steel stood in front of me. He didn't tell me well done, just stroked his chin, nodded and moved on. Two failed the shoot, Heaton and Jock, who would fire again. In the meantime the rest of us all moved back to the five hundred yard firing point as we did so we could hear Heaton and Jock firing again. Jock scraped through with a sixty-one. Heaton failed and would have to come back another day.

At five hundred yards we had thirty-six rounds each. We would have six exposures of the target of ten seconds each. We went through the same routine. To me it was like trying to hit a cigarette packet a hundred yards away. Jock failed to pass again. Peter scored eighty-one percent. I scored eighty-seven percent. "You fired a rifle before?" Sgt Steel asked me. "No, Sgt!" I replied.

"You seem to have an eye for it" he told me. ""Those are Marksman scores".

"Thank you Sgt." I replied.

Tuesday, with the Bren Gun, the results were much similar. We zeroed in at two hundred yards and carried out the shoots from five hundred yards and one thousand yards. I tried to keep my bursts down to two or three rounds, four at the very most. I knew that if I fired longer bursts of six or more my weapon would move off centre and my score would go down accordingly. At the end of two hours with the Bren my average score was eighty-seven percent. Peter was close behind at eighty-five percent. The next closest was around seventy-five percent. Both Peter and I had both classified again as Marksmen.

On Wednesday, for the SMG, we remained in camp on the small fifty yard range. The SMG was designed for urban, house to house, close fighting and was not that accurate above thirty meters. The targets were much smaller, showing only the head and shoulders of a man. The procedure was the same as on the large range except that we would commence at the fifty yard point and walk slowly forward until we reached the twenty-five yard point. At irregular intervals the targets would be revealed. Instead of popping up, as they did on the large ranges, they would already be up sideways on, and turned towards you to reveal the target. We only had three seconds for each exposure.

All went well for me until I got to the thirty yard point were I had a jam. By the time I had cleared the jam the targets had been turned away from me. Moving forward to the twenty-five yard point I had at least six rounds remaining as opposed to the three I needed for the last target exposure.

I had lost count and wasn't a hundred percent sure how many rounds I had left. At twenty-five yards the target swiveled to face me. I dropped to one knee. Aimed. Held my breath and gave two short bursts before the target turned away. I was certain I had at least two, probably three, rounds remaining. I was frustrated at having had the jam earlier. I lowered the barrel, took careful aim at the two by one piece of timber holding up the target. I squeezed off my final burst. Three rounds. A dull click informing that indeed I was now out of ammunition.

"Who the bloody 'ell was that?" Sgt Steel screamed, walking down the line. "Who fired after the targets had gone down?" No one answered. "For inspection port arms" he shouted. We cocked our SMGs and removed the magazines. Sgt Steel went along the line inspecting each and ensuring weapons and magazines were empty.

"Now" he went on "I want to know who gave a burst after the targets went down?" Silence.

"Well?" he bellowed. I raised my hand. "I should have known!" he sighed. "I had a jam," I told him. "So?"

"So, I wanted to make sure I qualified" I moaned.

"What were you shooting at?" he asked "pigeons?"

"The wood holding the target" I told him referring to the two by one inch piece of wood that the target was fixed to.

"Don't tell me you thought you could hit that from here" he asked.

"I could try!" I replied, sounding bolder than I actually felt.

There was a slight creaking sound from behind Sgt Steel. "Hey, Sgt, look at that", said Peter who was in the next lane to me. Sgt Steel turned to look down the range. I had to lean to my left to see what Peter was referring to. My target was leaning slightly to the right. At the five past twelve position. We watched as it slowly moved past the ten past twelve to quarter past twelve position before gravity finally took over and it fell to the ground.

We walked down the range to inspect our targets. Sgt Steel picked up mine from the ground. You could see two full half moon shapes where the rounds had gone clean through and a third right bracket shape on the left hand edge. The three rounds had effectively cut the piece of wood in half.

"If I hadn't seen it with me own eyes I'd never have believed it!" declared Sgt Steel.

"Will these three rounds count then Sgt?" I asked.

"No they 'effin won't" he replied, "They are not in the target".

That evening when we checked our scores I found that Sgt Steel had counted that last burst and I was a Marksman three times over, as was Peter. In fact Peter beat me by one with the SMG. I put it down to getting flustered when I had the jam. After dinner that evening Peter and I were given four cloth marksman badges to be sewn on to our uniforms. Later that evening I decided now was a good a time as any. I got out my needle and cotton to sew the badges on to my pullover. They had to be sewn on the right sleeve just above the wrist.

Peter had gone to the NAAFI with a couple of others for a game of pool. I was not good with a needle and cotton and it was difficult to get them lined up properly on my sleeve and had to put the pullover on two or three times to check the badges were nice and level. The first two were done and I had lined up and pinned the third when the Corporal sauntered in.

"Hello, Houghton" he said "What you up to?"

"Sewing on my Marksman badges," I replied. He looked at me and laughed. "What on earth are you doing?" he asked again. I pointed to the first badge on my sleeve. "Bren Gun" I said. Pointing to the badge above that. "SLR, and this one" I told him indicating the one I had just pinned and about to sew on. "Is for the SMG, and the last one, on the bed, must be a spare one!"

"Oh, you are a bloody pillock, Houghton!" the Corporal told me removing his stick from under his arm. "This one" he said, pointing at the first one I had sewn on "is correct!"

"This one" he said, pointing at the one above that, "is for your Battle Dress Tunic""

"This one" he said, pointing at the one I had pinned and started to sew on "Is for your Denim Jacket. And the one on the bed is for your combat Jacket!"

"I thought I got a badge for each weapon I qualified as a Marksman in!" I said.

"No! Don't matter how many weapons you qualify as a marksman in, you still only get one Marksman badge, you numbskull!"

"Oh!" I replied.

"One for each pullover and jacket!" the Cpl confirmed "I would unpick those two before anyone else sees what you've done, you'll be a laughing stock!"

Although embarrassed I was glad the Cpl had come in when he had. I could just imagine how I would have looked the next morning with three marksman badges sewn all the way up my left arm!

On Thursday morning several of the lads, Heaton and Jock amongst them, had to spend the day on the ranges to ensure they completed Basic. The remainder of us had several periods of drill practicing for a parade to take place at eleven thirty on Friday to commemorate the completion of our four-week basic training. From next week we would start our Combat Engineer training. After breakfast I was told that I had to again report to the medical officer for a check up at eleven o'clock.

As I did before, I went to the NAAFI at ten thirty and ate a hearty snack. A Steak and Kidney Pie with onion gravy followed by two cheese and onion crispy cobs and a mug of tea. Back on the scales in the Medical Officer's office I weighed eight stone two pounds! The Medical Officer was satisfied that I was now above the minimum weight, even if it was only by two pounds, and declared I need not visit him again. Having made use of the facilities in the Medical Centre before returning to the NAAFI I took out a penny and weighed myself again. I was back down to Seven Stone Twelve, fully clothed!

Thursday evening I was very pleased to learn that both Heaton and Jock had scraped through the ranges although several others, from other rooms, had still failed and would be back partied by two weeks. Poor fellows.

Friday morning arrived and we spent the first two hours after breakfast putting a final 'bull' shine on our best boots and putting the finishing touches to our Battle Dress Uniforms in readiness for the parade at 11.30 a.m. Sgt Steel and the Room Cpl fussed over us picking at this and that and making sure that we were as good as we could be. Sgt Steel was not impressed with the way I had put on my tie.

"Don't you know how to put a tie on Houghton?" He asked.

"Never had one before, Sgt?" I told him. He pulled apart my tie and began to tie it for me.

"It's like 'aving a bunch of kids who can't dress themselves properly" He declared. "There, that's more like it!" he continued, standing back to admire his handiwork.

"Thanks Pops!" I told him gratefully.

"Don't push it, Houghton!" He murmured.

At 10.30 a.m. we moved onto the parade ground for a last dress rehearsal. This time it was with the Royal Engineer Band. It was really exhilarating marching around the parade ground with the band for the first time. I was really beginning to believe I really could make it. In fact I had made it through basic, God knows how, I just had another thirteen weeks of combat engineering to endure before truly passing out as a fully fledged

Sapper. The parade itself was not for long. It took about half an hour. The Lt-Colonel taking the salute, I noticed, was the same one who had presided at the Court of Inquiry the previous Friday. We marched in file, in column a route, in line abreast.

In front of the Lt-Colonel we presented arms followed by the first verse of 'God Save the Queen'. Then Lt Mortimer marched to the front, saluted with his sword, and had a few words with the Lt-Colonel. Having done so he did a smart about turn to face the Training Party. Sgt Steel, who had been standing to attention behind us, did a smart right turn and marched around to stand next to Lt Mortimer. The Lt-Colonel came down from the saluting dais to join them. Then something I had not expected.

Two of the Training Corporals marched onto the parade ground carrying a small table covered with the Royal Engineer Flag. Lt Mortimer lifted a clipboard from the table.

"Best at Drill, Recruit Sapper Smith" he called out.

Smith, who was the one who had a nasty experience with a bed sheet, came to attention and marched forward coming to attention a few paces in front of the little table. The Lt-Colonel presented him with a Drill Cane, the same as those carried by the Training Corporals. They exchanged a word or two before Smith saluted, did a smart about turn and returned to the parade.

Other presentations followed in similar fashion, but presented with certificates. There were certificates for 'Best Turned Out', 'Best at Fitness', which left me out for a start. Then to my utter surprise, he called out.

'Most Improved Recruit, Recruit Sapper Houghton!" I was stunned. I froze for a second or two, and could see Sgt Steel looking at me as if to say "Come on! You Moron!"

I jumped to attention and marched out and came to a halt in front of the Lt-Colonel.

"Ah Sapper Houghton" he said, "We meet again!"

"Yes, sir" I replied.

"I am told by your Troop Officer and Troop Sergeant that they did not expect you to reach half this far".

"No Sir, I mean Yes Sir! Didn't they, Sir?" I stammered. I was totally shell-shocked and blabbering like an idiot!

"It is a credit to you that you have stuck it out and that you have really worked hard!" He went on. "Your fitness has improved one hundred percent!"

"Yeah, I thought to myself, like beating up Provost Sgts and losing Bren Guns!"

"Thank you, Sir," I replied aloud.

"Keep up the good work!" he said putting out his hand. I shook it. He then handed me an A4 Certificate, which declared in big gold, letters "Most Improved Recruit" and my name in calligraphy below it. Sgt Steel took the Certificate from me and I carried out a fair to middling salute, an ever so slightly wobbly about turn, and marched back to my position.

"Best Overall Marksman", bellowed Lt Mortimer "Recruit Sapper Houghton".

"Oh my god" I thought to myself "Twice!" I came to attention and again marched and came to attention in front of the Lt-Colonel. I saluted.

"Well young man, your averages on the rifle range are quite remarkable I see!"

"Yes, Sir!"

"You might like to represent the under 21's at Bisley next year?"

"Yes, Sir!"

"Very Well done!" he declared putting out his hand again. I shook it. He gave me another A4 Certificate declaring "Best Marksman" which I surrendered to Sgt Steel before carrying out another, even wobblier about turn and marching back to my position. Lastly came the highest award 'Best All Round Recruit' this went to Peter Duncan-Forbes who, in my mind, was the most deserving, for which he was presented a silver cup.

Back in Room 1, Spider 10 Sgt Steel came into the room with the Room Cpl. We had not failed to realize that all the presentations had been given to those in Room 1. This was due, in no small measure, to our Room Cpl and to Sgt Steel. As they walked in Sgt Steel dropped a cardboard box onto my bed that being the first bed he came to.

"Well my lads" declared Sgt Steel "That's your Basic Training over. You now have a hard thirteen weeks of combat engineering to come, if you continue to work as hard as you did during the last four weeks, I know you will do well!"

"Thank you, Sgt," we shouted.

"I can't hear you!" he bellowed back, laughing.

"Thank you, Sgt" we screamed again. The Cpl stepped forward. "Right lads, you have the rest of the day to yourselves, those of you who are allowed can have a good night out Saturday, but remember you have to be back in camp by ten p.m. and steer clear of any trouble, in the meantime" he said pushing out his hand towards the cardboard box "This is for those NOT allowed out!" With that he and Sgt Steel did a smart about turn and marched from the room, slamming the door behind them.

We all made a mad scramble for the cardboard box ripping it apart. Inside were three five pint cans of Courage Bitter and a can opener! Within no time at all our pint pots were out and the beer was flowing freely.

Chapter 13
THE DRIVING INSTRUCTOR
FROM HELL

As I had declared an interest in becoming a Plant Operator or a Driver Signaler I would obviously have to learn to drive. I was ordered on Monday morning, first thing, to report to the Driver Training Squadron on the other side of the camp. There I was introduced to my Driving Instructor Mr. Heatherton. 'Ton' being the operative term! He was hugely fat with several double chins and a girth, which placed a heavy burden on the buttons of his jacket that were in danger of 'popping off' every time he breathed out. In order to complete my driver training over the next four to six weeks I had to give up the first one or two training periods of my combat engineer training each morning and would therefore have to rely on a certain amount of homework to keep up with my contemporaries.

"You drove before?" Heatherton wheezed at me, as we walked onto large car park on which there where a large assortment of army vehicles.

"No, Sir" I replied.

"Cut the Sir shit!" he said, "Mr. Heatherton is my name".

"Yes, Mr. Heatherton".

We stopped by a large one ton truck. He threw me a set of keys. "Get in" he ordered.

Inside the cab we went through the vehicles controls.

"Clutch, Brake, Accelerator, Lights, Indicators, Choke".

"Start her up," he ordered.

It took two or three turns of the ignition key to get the truck to splutter into life. It sounded like a tank. It made a terrible racket. I could hardly hear what Heatherton was saying.

"Pay attention, boy!" he growled. "Dip your clutch" I dipped the clutch. "Into first gear". I moved the gear stick into first with a loud grinding chunk.

"Ease off the clutch, slowly, slowly until you can feel the clutch bite!"

There were several lurches forward, with such force Mr. Heatherton's head was bobbing up and down on his several chins.

"D-D-dip Y-Y-Your C-C-Clutch" he shouted as we kangarooed several yards forward.

"Into neutral, handbrake on!" he shouted, then "I can see I've got my work cut out with you, boy!" he told me. We repeated the process several times, actually hopping our way clear of the parking space.

On the fourth attempt, I had sussed it, and we were away. Speeding along at 5 mph around the car park. We stopped and started half a dozen times until I could actually come to a halt without stalling the truck or moving off again without actually leaving the ground. Finally after about an hour we moved serenely around the car park. I actually moved up into second gear speeding along at a neck breaking speed of 15 - 20 mph. To use the gears on this old truck you had to dip your clutch, move into neutral, dip the clutch again, and then move into the higher gear. Heatherton called it "Double-d-clutching".

It made changing gear that much smoother, he explained. "Enough for one day" Heatherton told me, wiping his sweaty brow, you be back here same time tomorrow. Back in my room my mates were covered from head to toe in mud.

"What have you lot been up to today?" I asked them.

"Digging field defences" they told me "and lining them with corrugated sheeting, we're making underground entrenchments, revetments and things". I told them about my first hour's driver training and fatty Heatherton. They were envious of my driver training. The remainder of the day I spent with my mates continuing to build our revetments. By the end of the morning I was as muddy as they had been at 11 o'clock. Sgt Steel asked me how I had got on during my first period of driver training.

"OK, I think". I told him "Mr. Heatherton is my instructor".

"Not that 'ol blob of lard?" Sgt Steel declared, "He's as tight as a ducks arse, so watch him, his pockets are so deep he can't reach the bottom!" Being so naive I was not quite sure what on earth he was on about.

Monday afternoon was far more interesting. Playing with anti-personnel and anti-tank mines in the classroom. Learning how to arm and disarm arm them and the various standard patterns they were laid in. Lovely stuff! This was more like it. This week I learned, would all be about mines and booby traps. It was a pity that I would miss the first training sessions each morning. But it would be worth it to get my driving licence at the end of it I supposed. Tuesday, after the first five minutes hiccupping around the car park, I was off around the camp. Within half an hour I was using third gear. Then, to my surprise, Heatherton directed me to the camp gates and before I knew it we were out on the public road.

We drove for about ten or fifteen minutes towards Cove before we came to a café on the outskirts of the village. "Pull in here" Heatherton ordered me. I did so turning a full circle so that I did not have to reverse the truck when we left.

"Lets have a quick cuppa, boy," he told me, opening his passenger door and squeezing himself out. We went into the café.

"Tea!" he ordered "and a couple of rounds of toast". I went to order the tea and toast. I realized that I did not have enough money on me to pay for my toast as well so I had to settle for just the tea. We sat in the Café for about twenty minutes. Then, burping and rubbing his massive girth, he suggested we make a move. Ten or so minutes later we were back in the camp and parking up. "See you tomorrow" he declared, waddling his way back across the car park. I was not very happy about spending one and six on his tea and toast. This must be what Sgt Steel had warned me about!

The rest of Tuesday was far more interesting. We learned all about booby traps and how to use them. Late that afternoon we were taken to an area of the camp that contained a number of defunct military equipment. We were told to booby trap them and the Training Cpl would try and find and defuse them.

We used small pieces of gun cotton as the explosive. If the booby traps went off they would make a reasonably loud bang. Jock managed to set his off before he had got the thing laid properly much to our amusement and the Cpl's anger. I was given an ex World War I, 50 pounder Field Gun, and a pressure switch. I walked around the Field Gun a few times trying to find a suitable place for a pressure switch. You obviously had to press the switch to trip it. The most obvious places were in front or behind the wheels or inside the breach block somehow. It was apparent that the Training Cpls had carried out this exercise many times and I would have to be a genius to figure out a suitable trap.

Stepping back from the Field Gun I looked around. The area of the gun was well trodden from much use. A little further afield I saw a small clump of dandelions. I dug out a small hole a couple of feet away from the rear of the Field Gun. Walked over and dug up the dandelions. I carefully placed my pressure switch, with its igniter and piece of Gun-Cotton into the hole. I then gently placed the dandelions into the hole over the top of my booby trap. I spread a little of the surrounding top soil around it so that the Dandelions looked as though they had been there all the time. The hole where the Dandelions had been I disguised with a couple of bricks. The Training Cpl moved amongst the relics the lads had booby-trapped. Most he found within seconds and quickly defused them muttering, "You could do better than that" or "Why didn't you try this?" giving advice as he went.

Then it was my turn. "Now what have we here?" He asked. "Pressure switch" I told him. He checked in front and behind the wheels as the most obvious. Then he started to examine the rear of the Field Gun more closely, peering at the breech.

"You have hidden this one well, Houghton" he said moving back a couple of feet, his head moving from side to side to look at the Field Gun from different angles.

I stood there holding my breath, bursting with sheer excitement and anticipation as his feet moved around my little Dandelion. "Very good, Houghton, you've disguised it well!" He was beginning to look frustrated. Then. "OK, Houghton!" he said, "What have you . . . " KERBLAM! Even though I was watching his feet and expecting the noise, it made me jump. The Cpl jumped several feet into the air, his feet dancing about giving a passable impression of a highland dance. He looked around frantically. My poor dandelions disappeared in a puff of smoke, their little leaves scattering around the Cpl's feet. " . . . done with it!" he finished lamely.

Everyone stopped and stared, then after a moment's shocked silence, broke into hilarious laughter. The Cpl went red in the face and looked fit to burst with indignation. There were cheers and jubilation amongst the lads. "Good on yer, Ricky" someone shouted. "One way of getting legless Cpl" Heaton mocked. The Cpl was not amused.

"You were told to booby trap the damn Gun!" he shouted at me.

"The Gun is no good without a Gunner, you're dead!" I told him.

"Never mind that, why didn't you do as your told" he bellowed.

"Only two places to put it," I said "either by the wheels or in the breech, you checked those two places straight away".

With great reluctance he conceded. "Well done, Houghton, first time I've been caught out - ever!" he told me grinning sheepishly.

"First time for everything Cpl," I said.

"Don't get cocky with me, Houghton, or I'll 'ave your guts for garters!"

Wednesday arrived. Mr. Heatherton was even grumpier that usual. I drove round the camp without a single kangaroo hop or without stalling once. Again we left the camp and this time drove for about half an hour. The only words I received from my illustrious driving instructor were, "take the next left" or "turn right at the next junction", other than that, silence. Eventually we arrived at the same café we had visited yesterday. Before Mr. Heatherton could say a word, "Am bursting", I told him "Dying for a pee!" I jumping from the cab trotted off and into the Café.

When I came out of the toilets Mr. Heatherton was sitting at the same table as before. He had not bothered to get himself a tea or toast. There were some bacon sandwiches in the glass hot cupboard next to the counter. "Can I have a mug of tea please and one of those bacon sandwiches". I asked the lady behind the counter. Taking my tea and sandwich I walked over to Mr. Heatherton and sat down.

Taking a huge bite of my bacon sandwich, and with a full mouth asked him, "Not hungry today Mr. Heatherton?" then picking up my tea took a long noisy slurp. "Hmm, lovely cuppa" I informed him. Mr. Heatherton flung his chair back and with a look that could kill proceeded to buy himself a cup of tea and two rounds of toast. We ate in silence. Finally he got up and with a nod of his head ordered me back on the road. We drove back to camp in silence. You could have cut the atmosphere with a knife. Once parked we both got out the cab.

"I am not sure I like your attitude, boy," he informed me.

"I am sorry" I replied, "Why's that, Mr. Heatherton?"

"You are insolent!" he told me, raising his voice.

"Insolent? I haven't said anything to you!" I replied, rising my voice to match his.

"You are a terrible driver, uncouth and rude!" he shouted.

"You are a terrible instructor and a fat overgrown slob!" I shouted back. He turned and stomped off.

In a temper I stormed after him and straight to the MT Officer's Office. I knocked on the door and was told to enter. A middle aged Captain sat at his desk with a cup of tea and smoking a woodbine. I could see the packet next to a full and overflowing ashtray.

"I am Sapper Houghton," I informed him.

"I know who you are Sapper Houghton" he replied.

"I would like to know if it is possible to have a different driving instructor." I asked.

"Why?" he queried.

"I don't think Mr. Heatherton and I get on very well," I said.

"You can't get on with everyone in this life my lad" he replied, "All the other instructors are allocated".

"I see" I replied, "Will another instructor become available later on?"

"Possibly, maybe in a week or two".

"Could I change then?" I asked him, but thinking to myself, "That's if I could stick it out with Heatherton that long!"

"Possibly, in a week or two" he repeated. I gave the Captain a salute, turned about and left. As I made my way from the MT area I saw Mr. Heatherton standing talking to two or three other instructors. He nodded towards me so I knew I was the topic of conversation.

I put Heatherton out of my mind for the rest of the day. Most of the afternoon training was in classrooms giving talks about bridging, the MGB (Medium Girder Bridge, the HGB (Heavy Girder Bridge and the HGOB (Heavy Girder Over Bridge) all of which we would have to build and dismantle, probably more than once, over the next two or three weeks. There were models set out on tables around the classroom and we were instructed on every piece of bridge from nose cone to panel pin.

Back at Spider 10 I made up my mind to talk to Sgt Steel about what had happened. I doubted I could sit in the same cab as Mr. Heatherton for another three weeks. "Don't know if there is anything I can do to help you," he told me. "The MT Squadron is a law unto itself and your Mr. Heatherton is a nasty piece of work!"

"Well if everyone knows that" I told Sgt Steel, "then they should understand why I don't want him as my instructor".

"Heatherton has been here for donkey's years" Sgt Steel informed me, "thinks he owns the place, plus he's on a new five year contract, so he knows he's on safe ground".

I felt gutted. This fat old man was going to ruin my ambitions to be a Plant Operator or Driver Signaler.

"I'll put the word out" said Sgt Steel, "See what can be done". "Thanks, Sgt" I told him. I had not felt so down since I arrived as I did at that moment.

Thursday. I made my way to the MT Squadron with trepidation. I was not looking forward to meeting Heatherton again. I need not have to worry about that I found out. When I got to my truck there was another driving instructor waiting there.

My spirits rose. Had Sgt Steel managed to pull a few strings? Then I saw he had a student with him.

"You Houghton?" he asked.

"Yes, Sir" I answered.

"You're wanted by the MT Officer, in his office". I turned and walked across the vehicle park to the MT Office. In the corridor was Mr. Heatherton.

"Been crying on your Troop Sgt's shoulder have you" he gloated. I didn't answer him. I walked up the corridor a yard or two to the Captain's office.

"Well you aren't coming out with me again" he sneered, "You little shit!"

I knocked on the MT Officers door.

"Enter" the Captain called and in I went.

"Sit down" he told me. I sat down.

"I have a problem young Houghton" he said. "Mr. Heatherton refuses to take you out driving".

"Did he say why?" I asked.

"Said you were not suited to driving, a danger to yourself, him and the public," I was told.

I told the Captain everything that had happened.

"It is him that is rude and arrogant" I finished off by saying.

"I sympathise lad", he said "But I still have a problem. If Heatherton refuses to take you out, none of the other instructors will either!"

"You are the Officer Commanding here" I said, "shouldn't these civilians you are employing do as they are told?" I realized immediately my mistake. The Captain didn't like that. He took a woodbine cigarette from the packet on his desk and lit it, puffing a ring of smoke above my head.

"Look lad, you can still do your driver training later, once you have been posted to your first unit, every Regiment runs driver courses in house, you'll just have to be patient" he told me.

"You mean I cannot carry on here?"

"'Afraid not lad" he informed me.

Without a word I got up and left, slamming the door as loudly as I dared. Heatherton was still in the corridor as I left.

"Be seeing you squirt," he remarked as I walked passed him.

"Not if I see you first you fat lump of lard" I sneered back.

"Dickhead" he shouted.

"Moron" I shouted back.

Outside I walked across the vehicle park on my way back toward Spider 10. My truck was parked in its usual spot. I walked up to it and patted the bonnet.

"I pity you," I told the truck, very close to tears, "having to put up with that bastard every day!"

As I walked away I could swear I heard a responding gurgle from the unfortunate truck.

Chapter 14
THE BIG BANG AND THE TEA LEAF!

I made my way slowly back to Spider 10. I knew I should not have felt like I had failed, but I did. Maybe I should have bought the fat slob his tea and toast. However, I felt that I was in the right and that I was the victim! As I neared Spider 10 I did my best to shrug off the disappointment and to try to look on the bright side. Which was, I would now be able to concentrate solely on my combat engineer training alongside my mates? "Yeah" I told myself "That's where I belong, not driving around in a decrepit old truck" I laughed to myself aloud "Sorry truck!" I said apologetically.

Sgt Steel was waiting for me on the steps of the Spider as I approached. As soon as I saw him the disappointment and resentment came to the fore once more. I squeezed my eyes together to ward off impending tears. Before I could say anything Sgt Steel walked down the steps and gave me a pat on the shoulder.

"Don't take it to heart, Houghton my lad, you are a better man than that prat Heatherton by a long chalk," he told me.

"It shouldn't be allowed" I replied quietly.

"I know, I know, but you mark my words, he'll get his come uppance one of these days" he reassured me. Sgt Steel was right. The following year, in August, I heard from a young lad who had experienced much the same as I had with Heatherton, arrived in my unit.

He told me that the Captain who was there when I was there had since left the Army. The new OC, a Major, took an instant dislike to Heatherton. Thought he was an arrogant and conceited buffoon and a terrible instructor. Within weeks of the new OC's arrival Heatherton had been told to resign or be sacked. He resigned.

"The lads are out on the demolition range" Sgt Steel informed me, "I'll run you up after lunch, in the meantime" he said, holding out a training manual, read up Chapter 9 in this, its what they did in the class room this morning before they left, it will bring you up to speed".

"Thank you, Sgt," I said taking the book.

"Read it carefully, twice, and I'll see you here after lunch. OK?"

"OK, Sgt"

Within a second pat on the shoulder Sgt Steel walked passed me and off in the general direction I had come from. He told me, much later, that he had been to see the Captain in an effort to get me a new driving instructor and had told Heatherton exactly what he thought of him. Brilliant. I read Chapter 9 of the training manual Sgt Steel had given me. It was all about cutting a four foot piece of railway line neatly in two using plastic explosive, PE 808, Great! I could not wait to get out on the demolition range to have a go. I read through Chapter 9 two or three times before my appetite got the better of me and I decided I needed something to eat. While I was at the NAAFI I decided to go and spend a penny, to check my weight.

I was eight stone and a few ounces. That's without cheating, I had had nothing since breakfast, so to celebrate I bought a cheese and onion cob and a glass of coke while I waited for lunch, which was still an hour away.

After lunch Sgt Steel met me outside Spider 10 at 1.30 p.m. in a Landrover as he promised.

"Hop in" he called. Off we went.

"Heard from Jamie?" He asked me.

"No, not really, we are not much for writing" I replied.

"Good lad your Jamie" he went on "We had some good times together me and him!"

"Oh" I asked

"Yeah, we did", said Sgt Steel, but he refused to go into any detail.

"A good man to have around" was all he said. It was only a half hour drive out to the range and when I got there the lads were receiving their final instructions from the Corporal about laying the charges to cut their railway lines in two. I jumped from he Landrover and joined the rest of my mates. They had formed a large semi-circle and were busy laying out their bits and pieces needed to prepare the charges.

"Ah, Houghton", the Cpl greeted me, "grab a piece of railway line and what else you need from over there" he told me pointing to one side of the semi-circle.

I grabbed hold of a piece of railway line, God it was heavy, and half carried half dragged it to the end of the semi-circle. "PE, detonators, igniters and detonation cord is what you need," the Cpl informed me. He could see I still held the Training Manual Sgt Steel had given me.

"You up to speed with this?" he asked, "Know what you're doing?" "Think so, Cpl" I responded. I kept an eye on those around me while the Cpl, in a no smoking area, sneaked off to one side for a crafty puff. I read the manual again. 'Take one ounce of PE'. Now I was stuck, how much does an ounce weigh? There was a good half a shoebox full of PE still left.

The PE was wrapped in brown paper, like sausages, about the size of half a ring of black pudding. Each packet, I guessed, must be an ounce. I took one packet, a detonator, some fuse wire and about three or four yards of fuse wire. Looking around I think everyone else had about the same.

I spent an enthusiastic twenty to twenty-five minutes preparing the charge, moulding the PE along each side of my piece of railway line. I inserted the detonator into the PE, from which I trailed the detonation cord a few yards out towards the centre of the semi-circle as others were doing. I attached an igniter to the end of the detonation cord. When ready, you pulled the little ring fastened to the igniter, this would light the detonation cord, which in turn would burn down to the detonator, which would, in turn, ignite the PE. Boom!

Checking everything over again very carefully and feeling satisfied I sat down, pulled my 'Commando' from the side pocket of my trousers, to wait for one or two of the other lads to finish. I heard the Cpl say, "Pull the pin out". I pulled the pin out and watched for a second or two as the detonation cord began to burn slowly towards the detonator.

"And only then, when I tell you to, pull the pin out" the Cpl went on, "I don't want any little girly screams and a mad dash for the safety bunker". I tried to replace the pin back into the igniter. The detonation cord continued to burn. "You will all walk calmly a quietly into the Safety Bunker, no running" the Cpl continued. It was at this moment, looking around the semi-circle, I suddenly realized that my charge seemed to be a lot bigger than everyone else's! I trotted over to the Cpl and tapped him on the shoulder.

"Now, pull the pin, this will ignite the demolition cord" he was saying, "and remember, don't run, walk!" I raised my pin up and into the Cpl's line of sight.

"I've already pulled my pin out," I informed him. There was a gasp from the lads. I saw Heaton cross himself enthusiastically. Must be catholic I remember thinking.

"Don't panic" the Cpl shouted out "Don't panic!"

"Where is your charge, Houghton?" he asked me.

"There", I said pointing off to the left, "the end one".

The Cpl followed my arm to where I was pointing.

"Jesus Christ!" he gasped "Run!" he screamed, already turning on his heels in a mad dash towards the bunker. We followed his example and all made a frantic mad dash for the Safety Bunker and just as the last man did a nosedive into the entrance there was a huge "Caboom!!" We felt the ground shake and could hear the soil falling back to earth, like huge chunks of hail on the corrugated roof of the Safety Bunker.

When we emerged from hiding and walked back up the slope to view the result, all we found was a crater, about twelve to fifteen yards across, a small puddle of water forming in the centre. There was not a single sign of any of the pieces of railway line anywhere to be found. My little extra large charge had also ignited the PE, which had been left, perfectly safely in normal circumstances, a little way off from where we had laid our charges.

"Houghton" the Cpl told me "You are a bloody jinx".

"I thought one packet was one ounce," I told him.

"They come in packets of six ounces you nitwit!" he informed me.

"Well how was I to know?" I asked, "You didn't tell me that"

"Don't you know how much an ounce weighs?"

"Of course I do" I said "An ounce!"

"You used at least six ounces!" the Cpl bellowed at me. "Sorry Cpl".

Then, stepping back, he declared "OK, we messed up, nobodies fault, nobody got hurt, lets leave it at that shall we?".

He knew that if word got out not only would I be in trouble, he would be in even greater trouble, we all nodded in agreement. The incentive was that we would all pass this stage of our demolition training. How could we not? It wasn't as if anyone could examine the pieces of railway line to see how we had done? As far as we could tell it had all been evaporated in the explosion. Back in camp we were asked, not just once, but a few times, what that large bang was this afternoon. Of course, we denied all knowledge.

"Wasn't us," we declared. But I was sure Sgt Steel had his suspicions even though he didn't press us for an explanation.

It was Friday at last. After PT we had several sessions of revision on mine warfare. Next week we would be out on Salisbury Plain laying and clearing minefields. I looked forward to that. Friday afternoon we spent carrying out our usual make and mend, washing, ironing, and generally getting ready for the week ahead. Four of the lads, now over eighteen, were planning on making full use of their first night out. However, the remainder of us was only allowed out until 7 p.m. Several others and myself decided it wasn't worth the expense of catching buses to Cove or Farnborough and remained in camp.

This weekend turned out to be the worst weekend of our five weeks in training. It started after dinner, about 7 p.m. when we were getting ready to either go out, or go to the NAAFI for a game of pool or a snack. Young Smith got the ball rolling. He came over to Peter and I and informed us that someone had stolen some money from his locker. We were devastated. We all trusted one another implicitly. Who would steal money from their own roommates? Peter confessed to having 'misplaced' some money the previous week. This select few, Peter, myself, Jock, Smith and Heaton had a little conference. "Mind you" I thought to myself

"It could be anyone, even one of our select few! I know it wasn't me; I still had two and half socks full tucked away. I knew it couldn't be my best mate, Peter, he was loaded.

We decided to lay a trap. I was the only one small enough in the room to be able to stand inside a locker and be able to look out through the three horizontal air slots a third of the way down each door. I was therefore, elected to be locked away from time to time, in Heaton's locker. His was fairly central and peering through had a good view of most of the lockers opposite. We did this at NAAFI break times and during meal times when we figured most rooms would be practically empty with hardly anybody about. It took three days. I must admit I was getting quite a bit fed up of being locked in Heaton's locker two or three times a day.

Wednesday morning. "Come on, Ricky!" Peter had said, "No-one about, time for a stint in the locker".

"Aw Pete", I moaned, "This isn't working, it's a farce, whoever nicked the money, it might have just been a one off!"

"Once a tea leaf, always a tea leaf" Peter declared, "Come on, we'll give you tomorrow off".

"Oh big deal!" I said stepping into the locker. Peter locked it and left, leaving the room's main door open; anyone passing would see there was no one in. I had been locked away for about twenty minutes, and wishing Peter would return to let me out, when I heard someone walk into the room. My initial reaction, thinking it was Peter, was to shout to him to get me out of here. But something stopped me; it was the way the person was walking in to the room, as if trying to soften his footsteps. I peered through the slots in the door. I could see someone but only from the neck down to his knees. He held a spoon in his hand.

He didn't walk too far into the room but went straight to Peter's locker. Peter's locker was on the same side of the room I was, so I could not see exactly what whoever it was, was doing. But I could hazard a good guess. Listening to metal on metal I assumed he was doing something with the spoon to force open Duncan's locker, like levering the top down to force the locks open. I was scarcely breathing. I could not identify the culprit. I hadn't seen his face. I heard Peter's locker doors suddenly spring open.

Heard the man rummage about for a minute or two. Using his spoon again he managed to lever and push the door back so that it was locked again. Then he made his mistake. He walked down the room a few yards to look through one of the end windows to check if anyone was coming. I didn't know his name, but I certainly recognized him, he was from room two. It was gratifying to know he was not from our own room. That evening, after Dinner, our whole room marched out and down the corridor and into Room Two. Inside we formed up as if on a parade.

The occupants, were all going about their normal business and in various forms of dress or undress stopped and stared at us in silence.

"What you lot want?" one of them asked standing up and walking toward us.

"Is he here?" Peter asked me quietly. I looked around.

"Can't see him" I replied.

"What's going on?" asked the man again. None of us answered.

"You just felt like paying us a social call or something?" the man asked.

Just then the door opened behind us and two lads walked in, one with a towel around him, and rubbing his hair with a hand towel. That was him.

"That's him" I informed Peter.

The man had stood stock still. He must have realized that something sinister was going on.

"Come in - have a seat," Peter told the tealeaf.

He sauntered in and walked to the end of the room and sat on his bed. He continued to dry his hair, eyeing us suspiciously.

"You have a thief in your room!" Peter announced dramatically. Even from where I was standing I saw the tealeaf go pale.

Peter informed the room about our loss of money and what we had done to catch the thief although he did not identify me as being the one in the locker. Any one could see, though, that I was about the smallest chap from Room 1.

"I have lost a bit too" Room Two's spokesman admitted, and so has one or two others.

"Who did you see breaking into your locker?" He asked.

"Chap on the end bed there" Peter said. All eyes swiveled to the end of the room where the lad sat, hands on his lap, staring back at us.

"This is a matter for Room Two" their spokesman declared. "We'll sort it out, you can stay" he told Peter.

"Rest of you can clear off!"

"I'll let you know what the score is lads" Peter told us "Off you go".

We all filed back to our own room. Although we were pleased for catching our thief, we were quiet;

there was no sense of jubilation or anything like that. I think we all just felt sorry for him. Half an hour or so later Peter returned. "They are going to hold a Kangaroo Court," he informed us.

"I don't like the sound of that!" I told Peter, "I think we ought to report it".

"He was given the choice", said Peter, of being reported to Sgt Steel, "or submitting to a Kangaroo Court, he didn't want to be reported"

"I still don't like the sound of it" I said.

"Me neither!" agreed Heaton.

"Nor me!" said Jock.

"Well let's see what happens," said Peter, "If we don't like it, we can report it".

"It might be too late then" I moaned.

"Let's wait and see" Peter said again.

Nothing did appear to have happened that night but when we were up the next morning getting ready for breakfast Smith came dashing back into the room toothbrush in hand and his mouth full of toothpaste, "That feller, the tea leaf, he's been beaten up, he's black and blue" he gasped, spraying toothpaste everywhere.

"Has he?" Peter asked, "Let's go see what's going on". Everyone who was in our room at the time, more than half of us, went to pay Room Two a second visit. When we walked in the same man who had been their spokesman the previous night stood in the centre of the room as if to block us going in any further.

"What's the score?" asked Peter.

"We found him guilty of thieving and bringing our room in to disrepute" he declared.

"And?" Peter asked.

"And he will get another thrashing on the next two Friday's" he told us.

I was beginning to dislike this man. He was obviously the room bully and was taking great pleasure in the situation. I could tell Peter didn't think much of him either.

"Once was enough" Peter told him.

"None of your business" the man said.

"It is our business and we say once was enough", Peter said firmly.

"It's what we, in Room Two, unanimously agreed" he told Peter.

Peter walked around him and walked to the end of the room. He stood looking at the tealeaf for a moment or two.

"Are you alright?" he asked him. The man didn't reply, just looked blankly back at Peter. Peter turned and said in a loud voice.

"So this is what you all agreed, unanimously?" he asked the room in general. He looked at each man in the room in turn. Most could not look him in they eye, lowering or turning their heads away. Peter walked slowly back up the room till he was standing toe to toe, eye to eye with the rooms spokesman. He spoke so quietly, even though I was just a couple feet away, I only just managed to catch what he said. "If this lad gets another beating, I promise you, I will be paying you another visit, but this time on my own and when there is no-one else around". I had never seen Peter so intense.

The other man couldn't hold his gaze any longer, lowering his eyes. "And believe me, you will not like that one bit!" Peter told him. With that Peter walked around the man and with a nod led us from the room.

We felt better, we were sure the tealeaf would be spared another beating, and after all it was Saturday. Although we had a pile of washing and ironing we knew a good night was in prospect. The few that were allowed out that night suddenly decided not to take up the offer. We all finished up, all twenty of us, taking the bus into Cove and spending a few hours wandering around the village. We made a collection and a couple went to the off-licence at the pub and bought a couple of crates of beer that we lugged down the road into a field. We made a square of several bales of hay and spent the next couple of hours telling jokes and stories as we drank the twenty-four bottles of Courage Bitter. After this we took the crates back to the pub. We couldn't get our money back on the bottles or the two crates because the pub had shut until six o'clock so we left them by the door.

Back at the camp, just in time for dinner, we planned a games evening, left side of the room versus the right side. We played dominoes, darts, pool and crib and didn't leave the NAAFI until it closed at ten o'clock. Immediately after breakfast on Sunday we concentrated on making sure the room was fit for inspection the next morning. We completed our washing and ironing. By mid morning more than half the lads decided on a second visit to Cove.

The remainder made a beeline for the NAAFI for their mid-morning snack. I decided to stay where I was. I thought about spending half an hour bulling my boots, but within five minutes was bored with that and took out my new 'Commando' comic that I had bought last night for a quick read.

Chapter 15
COCKTAILS ANYONE?

I had only be reading my comic for about five minutes or so when, from the corner of my eye, I saw a flash of red moving past one of the windows across the room. It was that damn Sgt with his Red Sash. "Why does he always come here?" I asked myself. I knew the answer. Spider 10 was the nearest Spider to the Guard Room. My room was the first room you came to when you entered. And my bed was the first bed you came to.

"Bad planning on my part", I thought. I stuffed the comic under my pillow and pulled the bed cover over my head. I would pretend to be asleep. I heard him open the door and walk in.

He stopped at the foot of my bed and tapped the end of my bed with his stick.

"You". He said.

I grunted and pretended to be in an even deeper sleep.

"You" he said again poking me in the ribs with his stick. I made a couple of grunting sounds before lifting the bed cover from my head. I did a passable mimic of being woken up from a deep sleep, rubbing my eyes and yawning loudly.

"Bugger off!" I told him, pretending I didn't know who it was. He let it go.

"What are you doing?" he asked me.

"Trying to sleep" I replied, "It's Sunday, you know, the day of rest".

"Got a little job for you" he said. I sighed loudly.

"Aw, Sgt, it's Sunday" I moaned at him.

"You get paid for it," he announced.

"Oh, how much?" suddenly interested.

"Don't know how much, depends on how well you do the job".

"What job?" I asked.

"Waiting on in the Colonel's house, afternoon cocktails, he needs a waiter!"

"Bit short notice isn't it," I asked.

"His usual waiter's father has died, he's had to go on compassionate leave," I was told.

"Bit inconsiderate dying before the Colonel's cocktail party" I moaned again.

"Less of that" ordered the Sgt, "Wear your Battle Dress Trousers and a clean shirt and tie, come on".

"I haven't said I want to do it," I said.

"I think you might need a haircut" the Sgt remarked, "and maybe your boots are dirty".

"And maybe you should give me a minute to get dressed" I responded.

"That's my boy" he replied, looking smug. "The Colonel's Staff Car is waiting at the Guard Room, be there in five minutes". He swiveled on his heals, stuffed his pace stick back under his arm, and marched smartly away.

Half an hour later I was standing at the back door to a massive house, must have half a dozen bedrooms, I thought. You could fit the whole of my house in Friar Park in his lounge. The Colonel opened the door. "Thank you for stepping in at short notice my boy" he said, waving me into this huge kitchen.

"My guests will be arriving any minute," he informed me; "now all you need to do is serve the wines". He waved his hand to indicate several cases of red and white wine. "Or prepare whatever they want, Gin & Tonic, Whisky, Brandy, it's all there" he said sweeping his hand along the counter. He swiveled around.

"And over here, there is the hors d'oeuvres"

"The horse-what?" I asked.

"The little snacks, just walk around passing them out".

"And later on, over there is a coffee percolator should any one want coffee". Just then the front door bell interrupted us. It was the sound of Big Ben was reverberating through the house.

"Don't worry, lad, you will be fine, any questions, just ask" and he left the kitchen and disappeared down the hall.

There was a babble of greetings and chatter as the arriving guests removed their coats and moved into the huge lounge. Each were offering each other various armchairs and seats as if they couldn't make their mind up where to sit. I busied myself pouring a mixed tray of red and white wine, stuffing my mouth with a couple of the snacks from the nearest tray as

I did so. I rearranged the tray so that it looked as if nothing had been taken. Finally they all appeared to have settled down and I went in with my tray of wine. They all appeared to be happy with a glass of wine; I only had one glass left when I returned to the kitchen. I swigged it down. "May as well make the most of it," I said to myself.

Now my dear old Dad didn't like the television much. Wasn't into football much either. He liked to watch 'Rawhide' 'Bonanza' and 'Saturday Night at the London Palladium' with Tommy Trinder, and later Bruce Forsyth and 'Beat the Clock. However, he did enjoy listening to classical music. Mozart, Beethoven and Schubert. One of his favourites was 'The Planets'. I had listened to it dozens of times and quite liked it myself. I would often lie in bed at night and listen to it wafting up the stairs and across the landing where my two brothers and I slept.

I helped myself to a biscuit full of little black balls and smelling like fish.

"Yuk!" I thought "'orrible stuff". There was a jar half full on the counter; the label read 'French Caviar'. The price label said one pound five shillings.

"Over a quid for that" I said aloud. "That is daylight robbery".

I took a bottle of red and white wine, one in each hand and moved back into the lounge, half filling my own glass first on the way. Having carried out a quick circuit topping glasses, the Colonel whispered. "Serve the hors d'oeuvres please".

"Pardon, Sir" I whispered back. Then drew back, suddenly worried in case he smelt that 'orrible fish stuff, and my wine.

"The snacks"

"Oh Yes, Sir, coming right up".

Returning to the kitchen I stuffed one of the hors d'oeuvres into my mouth and picked up two large trays and re-entered the lounge. Most of the guests did not acknowledge my presence as if the tray was floating around the room all by itself.

I think I received no more than an odd 'thank you' during the first hour. They talked in fairly hushed tones punctuated from time to time with "Jolly good show" and "I say old bean".

I had seen more life at a funeral wake. Most of my time I spent in the kitchen having the occasional tit-bit and sip of red wine. After that first hour I was beginning to feel a little flushed. "This is the life!" I told myself. I picked up another tray of goodies, "I 'spose I better go round again" I told myself aloud.

As I re-entered the lounge I heard that Colonel had put on a record. It was the 'Planets'. There was hope for them yet!

"Ah Venus!" I exclaimed, a little more loudly than I should have and waving my right hand in the air as if conducting the orchestra.

Suddenly all conversation stopped. All eyes were on me. It was as if I had walked back into the room with no clothes on.

"I say old bean" he said to me, the wine was apparently having and effect on him.

"You know this".

"Yes Sir" I replied, "of course, it's the Planets"

"You like classical music" he asked sounding incredulous.

"Yes, Sir, Mars is next, I like Mars, not sure which is my favourite though! Mars or Jupiter?"

I looked around the room. It looked like I had the floor. The party was becoming more interesting.

"Mars or Jupiter" the Colonel repeated.

"Yes, Sir" I said, stopping myself from picking up a glass of red wine from my own tray.

I spotted one or two leaning forward in their seats.

"Amazing!" said the Colonel shaking his head. Realizing they were expecting me to continue.

"I like the brass instruments and the drums in Mars, but in Jupiter they have a lovely string and wind section, quieter." The Colonel placed his empty wine glass on my tray and helped himself to another.

"'spose its what sort of mood you're in" I continued. "Mars would be good played as a March."

Venus had finished. Mars was next. I cocked my ear. "Mars" I informed my audience and began to subconsciously conduct the orchestra.

"Shall I turn it up a little?" I asked. The Colonel nodded.

They sat and watched me, thoroughly engrossed. The Brass Band was rising to a crescendo. I raised my finger pointing towards the ceiling.

"Listen, ready" they all leaned forward. I found that I was bending forward towards them, eyes raised to the ceiling.

"The drums" I whispered. Then as the drums joined the Brass Band I brought my finger down and across my body "Bum, bum, bum bum! I cried out. One or two jumped in their seats startled by my enthusiastic conducting.

"Ahem!" said the Colonel, looking flushed and raising his, yet again, empty glass. I looked down at my tray. It was empty. I gazed around the room. Most of their glasses were empty. I suddenly realized my glass was empty too, and I couldn't even remember having taken it. I beat a hasty retreat to the kitchen. I helped myself to a couple more hors d'oeuvres as I prepared another tray of drinks.

When I returned to the lounge the Colonel was saying. "And there was windowlene all down the front of his Service Dress . . . " he could hardly stop laughing. "And all over his shoes".

"Am I going to be plagued with this for the rest of my life?" I thought to myself as I continued to replace empty glasses with full ones. I returned to the kitchen and picked up the last two trays of 'snacks' and returned to the lounge. They had all gone stark staring bonkers.

"And then Mortimer and the Provost Sergeant" I thought the Colonel was going to have a heart attack!

" . . . Under the fence of the ammunition compound. . Ha ha ha!"

"an then he ran up with his pick axe handle". Everyone in the room was in hysterics.

The Colonel stood up and carried out an impressive simulation of my beating the Provost Sergeant about the head. He couldn't speak any more, tears streaming down his face, he fell back into his seat almost spilling his wine over his nice white shirt and wiping his eyes with the back of his hand.

"Sod it," I thought to myself "I'll leave them to it"

I put the full tray of drinks down onto the coffee table and returned to the kitchen. I sat myself on a stool, looked around, found a half-pint glass, and poured myself a generous glass of wine. I sat there sipping it and picking at the remnants of the snacks.

"Take a little back with you" the Colonel told me as he made his way past the kitchen door, "There is a carrier bag there somewhere".

I searched around, found the carrier bag, emptied the last of the snacks into a couple of serviettes, and then, checking that he was not on his way back, placed a bottle of wine in the bottom and the left over snacks on top. A little later I returned to the lounge to clear the empty glasses and the tray I had left behind. The doorbell sounded. "Oh I say," remarked the Colonel "That time already?"

The Officers in the room got up in a panic, smoothing down their clothes, wiping their mouths, and desperately tried to look stone sober. It was their wives back from their outing. As the door rang a second time the Colonel almost ran to open the door. "Hello darling, have a nice afternoon" I heard the Colonel ask.

"You look like you have!" a female voice retorted.

The guests began a rather hurried departure.

"Wonderful afternoon, Jolly splendid" one said.

"Absolutely spiffing old chap" said another.

"Must do this again old boy," said a third.

I saw the Colonel's wife give him a look that said "Over my dead body" as she walked passed him, removing her gloves and throwing them at the hat stand. She glared at me as if it was all my fault.

"Ahem!" said the Colonel, taking me by the arm and leading me hastily towards the front door.

"Ahem!" I said back. The Colonel pulled his wallet from his back pocket and opened it. There were several Five Pound Notes, Pound Notes and one solitary Ten Shilling note that I was sure he had saved for me. "Cor" Sir" I asked him "Those real Five Pound Notes?"

"They are," he declared.

"Never seen a real Five Pound note this close," I informed him.

"Well make the most of it lad," he said, "Because that's as close as you're going to get!" My nose was inches away from his wallet. He reached in and took the Ten Shilling note between thumb and forefinger.

"Ahem!" I said again. He looked at me, sighed and pulled out one of the One Pound notes. "Most generous, Sir" I told him, pulling the pound note from his reluctant grip,

"Thank you, Sir!"

Outside the Colonel's Staff Car was waiting and I walked, a little unsteadily, down the path and got into the car. It wasn't long and I was back in Room One, Spider 10, reflecting on a rather nice afternoon and holding up my pound note for everyone to see.

"Where you been?" asked Jock.

"Out!" I said.

"Out where?"

"Oh, just out" I said again, waving the pound note above my head. "Come-on, let's have it!" Peter told me. I related the whole story to my astounded roommates who bombarded me with questions.

"That'll teach you to abandon your mate and leave me here all on my lonesome" I told them.

I lifted up my carrier bag, took out the leftover's and the bottle of wine.

"Here you go fellers" I exclaimed. "A little treat"

"Bloody 'ell, Ricky" they shouted with glee "You're Ace!"

Pity we didn't have a corkscrew, had to ram the cork inside the bottle! But we got there.

Chapter 16
MUD, MUD, GLORIOUS MUD!

Sunday evening was terrible there was thunder and lightning, it literally poured down, the rain pounding our windows until the early hours keeping many of us awake. When we got up on Monday morning it was still raining. We had to make a mad dash to the cookhouse and back for our breakfast and returned to our room soaked to the skin. There were two little surprises for us that Monday morning. The first was that a list had been put up on the troop notice board asking us all to tick our preferences for leave at Christmas or the New Year. I think everyone in our room, with the exception of Jock, ticked Christmas. We knew that many of us would be disappointed, names would come out of the hat, and to see who could go home at Christmas and who would have to take leave over the New Year. I was hoping fervently that I would be able to take my leave at Christmas.

The second little surprise we had was when Sgt Steel came into the room for the morning inspection. After which he said.

"I don't know what went on last weekend and I don't want to know". He looked slowly around the room. "But I have a young lad who wants to move from his present room to this room, can't think why". We were a little non-plussed to say the least, who would want to move in here?

"He's from Room Two" Sgt Steel went on, "You might know him, uses the last bed down on the left".

We all knew then exactly whom he was referring to.

There was silence, no one responded to Sgt Steels question. "Give us a minute, Sgt" Peter asked.

Sgt Steel nodded and left the room.

"Well?" asked Peter.

"We don't want a tea leaf in our room" Heaton said. A few murmured their agreement.

"I look at it like this," said Peter "He's made a mistake, we all make mistakes, but we all deserve a second chance!"

"We don't make the mistake of thieving from our room mates" said Jock.

"If you say no Jock, its no!" Peter said, "Who else wants to deny this lad a break?"

Everyone looked to each other, waiting for each other to protest, nobody seemed to want to be the first to stop the tea leaf from moving into our room.

"Up to you Jock!" Peter told him, "If you say no mate, that's what I will tell Sgt Steel, we all have to agree one hundred percent!" Jock looked around him seeking some support. I could see that most of them were in two minds about what to do, but none wanted to be the first to say no.

"What shall I tell him, Jock?" Peter asked.

"I don't care!" replied Jock, "Tell him what you like".

"Any one else against the lad taking Riverton's bed?" Peter called out. No response. Peter walked out and told Sgt Steel it was OK. Half and hour later we trundled our way out to the bridging site on a three ton truck. The rain leaked around the canvas into the back of the truck. It was also very cold. When we arrived at the bridging site we found the bridge train, several ten ton trucks that carried the bridge, waiting for us. We were expected to have the bridge up and running within eight hours.

On the first of the trucks was the bridge nose cone, carrying handles, panel pins and first ten meters of MGB. We had been through the build in theory, putting into practice was another thing. The drivers of the bridge train had already removed the fastenings holding the components in place on the back of the trucks. Sgt Steel quickly organized us into two parties, left and right, and we got the build under way. Each panel was a four-man lift. The cross panels were huge, an eight man lift, and it was these that were positioned across the bridge to support the traffic. There was no let up from the rain and we were again soaked to the skin.

We quickly had the nose cone put together. The nose cone protruded some ten meters out from the front of the bridge, over the gap, to prevent the bridge dipping or falling down into the gap or river as the bridge progressed across the thirty meter gap. The first panels were in position, the pin man ramming the panel pins home at top and bottom of each panel to hold them into position.

We were doing well during the first two to three hours, making reasonable progress. However, the ground was becoming more and more muddy. The ground was fast being turned into a quagmire, which was making the carrying of the panels more and more difficult, and not a little hazardous, to carry. It became obvious to us all that we would not be able to complete the bridge in one day. Several times I got my boots firmly stuck, unable to move, at one point stuck half way between ankle and knee.

Most of the other guys, being that much taller and better built than I, coped far better. In the end I was taken off trying to lug the panels from truck to bridge because others were forever having to help me to pull either one or both of my feet from the thick mud.

At lunch time a Landrover turned up with several hay boxes, one of a welcome thick stew, a second with boiled potatoes and a third full of a mixture of cabbage, carrots and cauliflower. The last two contained trays of spotted dick and thick lumpy custard. There was also hot, and equally as thick and lumpy, gravy, several loaves and a huge urn of hot tea. Ignoring the rain we attacked this feast with utter relish. We had not realized just how hungry we had become, absolutely ravenous, and we made short work of the meal. I did manage to go round for a second helping of both the stew and the dessert. Even though both were now barely luke warm and much diluted by the rain, I scoffed the lot, soaking up any remnants I found with rain soaked soggy bread.

After our lunch we turned our attention once more to getting the bridge finished. We had no hope! At half passed two Sgt Steel called a halt. We had reached the far bank. However we still had to build the ramp section on the near side bank and of course to lay the surface of the bridge. The bridge build would be deemed a success when the bridge train had effectively driven from one side to the other. However, this would have to wait until tomorrow, by the end of which we should have dismantled the bridge and replaced it onto the trucks.

Sgt Steel dismissed the bridge train, telling the drivers to return at eight in the morning. He then ordered us to 'tidy up' the bridge site, stacking pin panel boxes and other bits and bobs neatly beside the bridge. He was going to return to camp and organize an early return of the three ton truck that had brought us to the site that morning. He jumped into his Landrover, and with much churning of mud and spinning of rear wheels, and with the help of a half a dozen of us pushing and shoving from behind, he left the bridge site for the camp.

Within minutes we had 'tidied up' the site as instructed. Somebody, either Jock or Heaton or both of them, decided to lob a ball of mud from one side of the bridge over to the other. It caught poor Smith smack on the back of his neck. We all found this highly amusing, Smith retaliated in similar style and within minutes our two teams, left and right, were engaged in all out war. Peter had the ingenious idea of pulling up tufts of grass by the roots and swinging it around his head, let it go with extreme accuracy, hitting poor Jock full in the face. Men were running around and climbing all over the bridge wielding great clods of turf or balls of mud and throwing them in all directions. We were having so much fun no one noticed the reappearance of Sgt Steel who had left his Landrover down the track someway for fear of getting stuck in the mud. All we heard was, "What the bloody hell's going on here? What are you doing?". Unfortunately for Sgt Steel, someone on the far side of the bridge whose ears must have been full of mud, let go with a fairly good sized tuft of grass.

There was a huge blob of mud still attached to its roots. It caught Sgt Steel smack on the side of his head. There was a brief cheer! He stood motionless, glaring at us. His face was a picture! I am fairly sure he couldn't decide whether to scream with rage or burst out laughing. Controlling himself he screamed.

"Get round here the lot of you, three ranks, move!"

Those on the other side of the bridge scrambled around and we formed up into three, very muddy, very wet, very dirty ranks.

"Just look at our lovely bridge", said Sgt Steel quietly. We all turned to look. There was literally tons of mud splattered all over it with tufts of grass caught in every conceivable crevice.

"Tomorrow morning you will bring half a dozen buckets and brooms and you will clean this bridge until its gleaming," he bellowed, "and you will stay here until the bridge is dismantled and back on the bridge train even if it takes you all night!" This was met with stony silence.

Sgt Steel paced up and down in front of us. We must have looked a pretty picture. We were soaked and covered from head to toe in mud. Peter and Jock, who had both caught a face full of mud, looked like something out of the 'Black and White minstrel show'. "You want to play do you?" asked Sgt Steel quietly. There was no response.

"I can't hear you," he shouted.

There was a mixed response of "No, Sgt" and "Yes, Sgt".

"Make your minds up!" he continued, "Looking at the state of you I think you do like to play!"

Sgt Steel then enjoyed the next half an hour marching us up and down, running on the spot, doing sit ups and press ups in the thick mud. Finally he had us roll down the bank into the gap, which by now contained several inches of muddy water. Then as we slipped and slid and struggled our way back up the bank we heard our three ton truck arriving. There was no better sight for sore eyes than this and we thankfully climbed aboard. Surprisingly, no sooner had the truck moved off, we burst into song, linking arms and swaying side to side as we went.

Our Sgt Steel Jumped from 40,000 feet
Our Sgt Steel Jumped from 40,000 feet
Our Sgt Steel Jumped from 40,000 feet
But he ain't gonna jump no moo-ore

He landed on the tarmac with a satisfying thud
He landed on the tarmac with a satisfying thud
He landed on the tarmac with a satisfying thud
And he ain't gonna jump no moo-re

They scraped him off the tarmac like a lump of
strawberry Jam!
They scraped him off the tarmac like a lump of
strawberry Jam!
They scraped him off the tarmac like a lump of
strawberry Jam!
And he ain't gonna jump no moo-re

Back at Spider 10 we were dismissed and trudged wearily into our room dripping and trailing mud, which would all have to be cleaned up, as we went. We stripped off and headed for the showers. Dinner time was fast approaching and we were starving.

We would also have to wash every item of clothing we had on that night and I knew access to the washroom would be at a premium. As I walked into our room we were met by an incredulous open- mouthed new arrival, it was Plaid, our tea leaf from room two.

"Bloody 'ell," he asked, "What happened to you lot?"

"Don't ask!" someone muttered.

Just at that moment there must have been a break in the cloud because the rain suddenly stopped and the sun came out bathing the room in sunshine! Peter walked to the window, opened it, thrust out his head and shouted at the sun,

"You're too bloody late, you wanker, where've you been all day?" This lightened the mood and Heaton confessed that it was he that had thrown the last tuft of grass, which caught Sgt Steel.

"Good shot eh?" At which we all had a good laugh.

Five minutes later all nineteen of us were cramming ourselves into the six available showers in order not to be late for dinner that was due to start any minute now.

Much later that evening myself, Peter, Jock and Heaton and our tea leaf Plaid were the only ones left in the room. Many of those in the room had not acknowledged Plaids presence as yet, choosing to ignore him, and it was plain to us that he was feeling uncomfortable. After a while he got up, walked to the centre of the room and coughed nervously. We turned to face him.

"Just want to thank you for backing me up" he said quietly. No one answered but I saw Peter give him a reassuring nod.

"And to say sorry for what I did" he said, a tremor in his voice. Still no one answered him.

"My Dad died last year" he went on, barely audible, "And I've got three little sisters and a baby brother, that's why I joined up".

"No excuse for thieving from your room mates", Jock said quietly, but unforgiving.

"They barely got enough to live on" he stammered, "and with Christmas coming, wanted to send my mom something". He got to his feet and pulled a wallet from his back pocket. Opening it he pulled out several Postal Order stubs and showed them to Peter. He had four pounds worth of Postal Orders.

"Sent this to Mom the afternoon", he looked at Peter, "the afternoon I broke into your locker".

"What would your mother think?" Peter asked him.

"She won't find out" he replied.

"What do you think she would think if she did?" Peter asked him again.

"She would take the broom to my back" he confirmed.

With a sigh Peter got up and taking young Plaid by the shoulders told him.

"But that's the end of it, right"

"I swear, on my mo . . . I swear it!" he said his lower lip trembling slightly.

"Well then," said Peter "That's an end to it".

"And thanks for letting me move in here, that idiot next door is making our lives a misery" said Plaid.

"He'll get what is due him in due course" Peter told him, "those sort always do!"

After a moments silence I asked no-one in particular, "Anyone for half an hour on the pool table?"

"Okay" replied Peter, "You coming?" he said to Plaid.

"If you like," he answered.

"Right, lets go!"

The three of us walked up to the NAAFI. Neither of us said a word.

That evening I raided my socks and removed four pounds, mostly in half crown pieces. I couldn't do anything the following day but on Wednesday I purchased four pounds worth of Postal Orders. As I was leaving the Post Office I almost bumped head on into Peter.

"Look were you going, Ricky" he said. He looked down at my hands,

"What you got there?" I don't know why but Peter read me like a book, I couldn't lie to him.

"Couple of two pound Postal Orders," I told him.

"What for?" he asked.

"Thought I'd leave them for Plaid, anonymous like" I replied.

"You can't afford to give four pounds away!" Peter said skeptically.

"If I couldn't, I wouldn't" I said.

Peter stood weighing me up for a moment or two.

"Your bloody mad, Ricky".

"I know" I replied laughing.

"And I am even crazier!" he said, unbuttoning his breast pocket. He fished out five pounds worth of premium bonds.

"Where shall we leave them?" he asked.

"We'll just stick them in an envelope and leave them under his pillow" I suggested.

"Yeah, we can blame the tooth fairy!" said Peter.

Laughing at our own generosity and good humour we walked back to the Spider. Later, while Plaid was briefly out of the room, Peter slipped the envelope under Plaids pillow. The next morning Plaid said nothing about his gift from the tooth fairy. We went on PT, had breakfast, and returned to our rooms, and still he said nothing. Plaid had made up his bed pack that morning so he could not have failed to find it.

Finally, while Plaid was again out of the room, Peter and I checked the top of his bed, nothing, but when we pulled the bed out, there it was on the floor propped against the wall.

"Bloody thing fell behind his bed" Peter said unnecessarily.

"What shall we do now?" I asked him.

"We'll leave it on top of his pillow this time". A number of those in the room gave us curious glances. Not all of them knew what we had been up to. "Keep your mouths shut!" Peter ordered. As Peter and I left, Plaid came back in. He found the envelope and opened it. He looked around the room hoping to find a clue to his unknown benefactor. We ignored him. Plaid spent the next few days grilling people and trying to find out who is benefactor was. Peter was an obvious candidate but he denied all knowledge just as I did. Believing that there could not have been any one person, which was true, Plaid came to the conclusion that the whole room and maybe others too, had contributed to his gift. He wrote a note of thanks 'To whom it may concern' and pinned it to the notice board. Nice touch that, I thought.

Plaid's sojourn in Room One was short lived. Just over a week later, in the gymnasium, he fell, breaking his arm. He was packed off on three weeks leave and when he returned he was ordered to pack up and move to Spider 10, to 126 Training Party. He had been back Partied a month. We still met from time to time in the NAAFI until, after he had been back five or six weeks, he disappeared. We heard later that he had left the Army. Apparently because his mother was having a rough time and needed him at home.

I hope my four pounds were put to good use!

Chapter 17
KEYSTONE COPS

I don't know where the next two weeks disappeared to. We were out most of those two weeks building, dismantling and rebuilding our MGB and HGB's. I must confess that at the end of those two weeks we were getting quite slick and could have an MGB up and running in about seven and a half hours. I did not get my wish for Christmas leave. My leave was to be from 27 December until the first Monday in the New Year. Nevertheless as my leave grew nearer I became more excited at the prospect of returning home. Really looking forward to it with growing enthusiasm. Christmas week was quiet. On Christmas morning I was awoken at eight by Lt Mortimer and Sgt Steel who dished out liberal quantities of black rum and heavy sticky mounds of

Christmas pudding smothered in lumpy custard. What a treat that was!

I had two Guard duties during Christmas, one on the 23 December and one on the 26 December. I took the opportunity of removing a full sock of silver coins from the culvert, leaving just the one remaining sock, which was about half full. I managed to convert a sock full of change into my first ever couple of five pound notes, three one pound notes and a ten bob note. I was going to go home filthy rich. On 26 December we were called to parade in the corridor outside the Troop Office. We were then called in to the Office in alphabetical order. We were being paid our credits.

Until then I had never heard of 'credits' and certainly didn't know I had accrued any. I learnt that, as we were under eighteen, part of our pay had been compulsorily deducted from our pay as a sort of savings. Apparently the Army believed we were incapable of saving up for periods of leave using our own initiative. They were probably right. However, I had accrued four pounds in credits since my arrival, for which I duly signed for. I was going home with close to twenty quid! I had never dreamed of ever having so much money at any one time. We were also issued with return rail and bus warrants to get us there and back.

At last the big day came. I had not told my family that I was coming on leave. I wanted to surprise them. During the Christmas period I had made enquiries about the train timings to make sure I would not get stuck on any mail trains. This took hours off my journey time. Wearing clothes mostly donated to me by Peter and packing a brand new small case, not much bigger than a briefcase.

In the briefcase I had a spare shirt and pullover, three pairs of brand new socks and, my family would never believe this, four pairs of brand new underpants. I would be dressed like Rockerfeller himself. One thing I neglected to buy was a cap. I had not thrown my old one away, which was my old school cap, for some sentimental reason and had packed that. It had a shield shape of darker cloth at the front which showed where my school badge had been.

I knew Wednesbury market sold cloth caps and vowed to buy me one as soon as I got home. I had also bought myself, a while ago now, a nice leather wallet. I also took with me my two certificates, for 'Most Improved Recruit' and 'Marksman' which I had folded and put in my inside pocket.

The journey home was uneventful. I found that I loved the travel. At one point I stood for an hour in the corridor, with the window down, letting the cold air blow my hair every which way. I kept putting my head out of the window from time to time to watch as the train sped its way through the countryside. Just as I stuck my head out of the window for the umpteenth time I did so just as a new diesel express train roared past. It frightened the living daylights out of me and from then on only stuck my head out after making sure nothing was coming the other way first. Diesel trains were still fairly new. Most of the local trains were still steam trains.

At last I arrived at Birmingham Snow Hill Station and was soon on my way by bus to Stone Cross. When I got to Stone Cross I suddenly had the idea of getting a taxi from there to my home, even though it was only a fifteen minute walk, I could arrive home in style. There was always a couple of taxi's parked close to the bus stop and enquired about the price. Three-and sixpence. Christ, that was a lot; I could get two pints of beer for that later! Having asked the price I felt foolish about not then using the taxi so I jumped in.

Five minutes later the taxi pulled up in front of my house, it looked remarkably unchanged, the front garden as overgrown as ever, the green paintwork peeling from the front door. I got out of the taxi, hoping someone in the house had seen me arrive, and paid the taxi driver. I added an extra 'thrupence' as an over generous tip! I walked up the path, finding the door unlocked, as it usually was in those days, marched in. There was no one in! I was gutted, I had wasted three and nine pence on that damn taxi! As soon as I walked into the house there was a damp musty smell, which I had not noticed before.

I stood in the centre of the living room taking in the scene. Dad's old leather armchair was to the right of the fireplace. It sagged in the middle and some of the yellow stuffing was peeking out from the sides. He had a tattered old flowery cushion he used to offset the dip in the middle of the seat. The two seater sofa was threadbare and ready for the skip. A home made carpet, made from sacking and strips of old clothing, covered the centre of the floor in front of the fire. I was seeing the house in a totally different light and felt a pang of sympathy for my family. I walked through the house and into the back yard. Marg, the old lady from next door, was taking in some washing. "Hello Ricky!" she called, flashing her gums. "Hello Marg" I responded, "How are you?"

"Mustn't grumble".

"Where is everyone"? I asked.

"Down the Cross, I think" she informed me. I couldn't believe it; I had just got a taxi from there.

"What time they leave?" I asked Marg.

"Not long" she said, "'bout half an hour ago!"

They must have arrived at the Cross five or ten minutes before I got the taxi. I dumped my 'suitcase' onto the sofa intending to walk back to the Cross. Just as I got to the bottom of my street I saw the number 11 bus moving up Crankhall Lane. I ran up to the bus stop and stuck out my arm. Five minutes later I was back outside the Cross.

Conscious that I was still under age, I went around the back to the lounge and walked in. There, at the same table I had sat at six or seven weeks earlier, was Muth, Dad, Kev and Don. Don spotted me immediately.

"Bugger me!" he shouted "Look what the cats dragged in!"

Seconds later Muth was trying desperately to break my neck. She hugged me with such force that I actually heard my neck creaking. Dad was instantly on his feet and at the bar calling to Harry for another round. Harry appeared and without a word began to pull the beers. The first one he handed across the bar to me. "First ones on the house", he said.

"Thanks" I told him taking the pint glass and went to sit down between Muth and Dad. There was a barrage of questions.

"Good Lord, Son" said Dad, "You've put a bit of weight on".

"Oh, have I? Hadn't noticed" I replied, vowing to go and weigh myself when I got the chance. I hadn't weighed myself in well over a week. I told the family about the windowlene, about the poor Provost Sergeant, and my run in with the lad in the NAAFI when I had been playing pool with Heaton.

I had embellished the stories somewhat and they were falling about themselves in laughter. I did not tell them about loosing my Bren Gun though. I told them all about my roommates and about Peter, my best mate. My family were genuinely pleased for me. They still could not really believe I had not been chucked out. Kev reminded me about my certificates by questioning me about rifles and such. I stood up, and with a flourish and a 'tarrahn' simulating a fanfare, I produced the certificates from my inside pocket. I handed them to Dad.

"Well done, Ricky" he said "looks like your doing alright".

"Bloody 'ell ah Kid" said Kev, admiring my marksman certificate, "I didn't think you could hit a barn door if you were standing on it!"

"These really yours?" They asked.

"Am a Houghton, remember," I told them, "Course they're mine".

They seemed genuinely impressed.

Needless to say the beer flowed and it was not long before both Kev and Don had got their rounds in. Using the Army as an excuse I patted my tummy and said, "Take it easy you lot!" I told them, "I have to watch my weight!" They all thought this was extremely funny and fell about laughing. But they got the message, and did not force the pace and allowed me to take my time. At twenty past two Harry called last orders. The bar closed at half past and we then had half an hours drinking up time. We had to vacate the premises by three. I went to the bar and ordered my first round; Dad,

Kev and Don had refused to allow me to by a drink up until then.

I also ordered a rum and pep, for Muth and three shots of Black & White Whisky for Dad and my brothers.

"Where's your short?" Kev asked. I didn't like the idea of having a whisky with my beer.

I patted my stomach again. "Watching my fitness," I told him. They still thought the idea of me worrying about my weight extremely funny but Dad tapped me on the shoulder saying "Good on you, Ricky".

Within minutes of the bar closing in walked 'Big Ears'. Big Ears was our local bobby and I had known him practically all my life. He had arrested me once for 'Breaking Broken Windows' on a derelict house and once when he had caught me down the cut (canal) shooting tiddlers I had caught with an air pistol. You had to be eighteen to own an air pistol but I had borrowed it from one of my neighbours to play cowboys and Indians with. I hadn't even had any pellets but was using the air from the pistol to blow the tiny fishes back into the cut. With Big Ears though it seldom went any further, most times he would give you a good clip round the ear and that would be the end of it. We didn't dare go home and tell our parents that Big Ears had given us a clip round the ear because in all likelihood you would get another one from them!

Don quickly jumped to his feet as soon as he saw him. "Afternoon, all" he announced.

"Would you like a half Constable?" Don asked politely. Big Ears looked across at me. He knew full well there was no way I could be eighteen until the following year.

"Ricky is in the Army" Don informed him, "Just got home on leave for the New Year".

"Well", said Big Ears rubbing his chin and peering at his watch. "I'm about to go off duty, very kind of you Don!" He turned to Harry saying. "A pint of your Best Bitter, Harry, if you don't mind". Best Bitter was two-pence a pint more than the M&B mild we were all drinking.

We made a point of drinking up fairly quickly and were making a move from the lounge a good five minutes before the end of drinking up time. I had not told them about my fiasco with the taxi claiming to have walked home and finding them not at home had walked back. I might have known I would be found out though, because a neighbour from across the street popped by later that afternoon claiming he had seen me arrive in a huge posh taxi. They gave me a hard time about wasting money on Taxi's in order to save such a short walk. At home I gave my mother four pound notes telling her that it was for my weeks keep. She objected at first, but at my insistence, pulled her purse from down her bra, safely lodged the notes in it, and pushed it back, giving it a affectionate tap to make sure it was secure.

The next few days just flew by. We were down the pub most lunchtimes and every evening. So much so that I really did begin to worry about my intake. I began to take my time with the beer even more. I asked to be left out of a couple of rounds during the course of the evening drinking sessions and I was grateful that they did not push me.

I had forgotten just how much my family could put away during the course of the night. They drank gallons of the stuff. I went to Wednesbury market and, although the market was not on, got me a pretty good flat cap for only nine and eleven pence.

I made a specific point to go and visit my schoolmate Ben. Regrettably he was not at home. His sister, Fiona, who was the same age as me and had been one of my class mates, informed me that he was now a 'Driver's Mate' with a long distance haulage company and travelled all over the country. I asked if he would be back during the next few days but she did not know when he might turn up or for how long. I left feeling a little disappointed at not being able to meet up with Ben.

Both Fiona and I were a little embarrassed to meet again, especially as she was in the house alone. We go way back, when we were just eleven or twelve years old. I had turned up at Ben's house to see if he was at home. The doors were not locked; they never were in those days. Finding no one at home, I was about to leave, but decided to go for a quick pee first. I went upstairs to the toilet and believing no-one was at home didn't bother closing the toilet door. While I was in the toilet I heard Fiona and another girl giggling in the bedroom next to the toilet. It was Ben's room. I believed at first they had found the noise I had made while relieving myself rather amusing. Buttoning up, I walked from the toilet and stood outside Ben's bedroom door. They were giggling and whispering together.

I suddenly pushed open the bedroom door,
"ha ha!" I cried, "What do you think is so funny?"
As I entered the room I saw Fiona's friend Julie, crush a magazine to her breast, trying to hide the cover from

me. I walked into the room and sat between them. "What have you got here?" I asked the girls. At first they refused to let me see, but I could see from the front cover that it was some sort of girlie magazine.

It didn't take much persuasion from me to convince them to let me have a peek. I had never seen anything like it in my whole life. It was very, very explicit. Looking at the lewd pictures in the magazine, in the presence of these two girls, was to say the least uncomfortable. Julie was very brazen, she was really enjoying my embarrassment. As I turned the pages nature, of course, was taking its natural course. Julie started the ball rolling. "Are you like that?" she asked pointing at a particularly large phallus. "No I'm not!" I replied indignantly.

I caught Julie making a grab, for what I thought at first, was the girlie magazine. I lifted it up, out of her reach, only to find her hand was directed at my lap! Not the magazine.

"He is hard!" she cried delightedly.

"Gerrroff!" I shouted back at her. "Leave me alone!"..

Julie wasn't to be denied. "Let's have a look," she asked.

"You must be joking" I replied aghast. Julie was pushing me back from my shoulders. The more she pushed, the more I felt my resistance weakening. Before I knew it her hands were busy with the buttons of my trousers.

I made a feeble effort to resist. Fiona, in the meantime, just sat there passively, she did not encourage Julie, but then again neither did she protest either. In the end I gave in to the inevitable. Julie had hauled my pants down to the knees. The two girls sat and stared at the humiliating display. Then Julie reached out and took a hold. It was like taking hold of an overheated champagne bottle. The moment her fingers took a hold of the neck of the bottle the cork popped. The two girls sat fascinated as they watched the fireworks. Julie took one of Ben's T-Shirts from the washing basket and began to mop up. "Do it again!" she demanded of me. "I can't," I informed her. "Can only do it once", then for the first time, Fiona spoke. In a whisper she said, "I think you have to jiggle it for a bit". Julie did not need to be told twice and, with a fierce grip and with an expression of sheer determination on her face she proceeded to open a second bottle of Champagne. After which, trousers still around my ankles, I made a mad dash for the stairs and freedom. For the rest of the week I wondered around with a silly smile on my face.

Back to the present. Thursday had arrived, New Years Eve, and we decided to go to West Bromwich to celebrate in style. We left early, about six o'clock, so we would be in the pub before it got too packed out. We were met at the pub by two or three of Kev and Dons mates. One of these was a chap called Joseph White from Jamaica. He was six foot twelve inches if he was an inch! He towered above Kev who was six foot something himself.

Joe was as black as coal and took great delight in telling people his name was White. He had a great sense of humour and was forever cracking jokes and making fun. At about ten o'clock that evening we left that pub to go to a posher pub across the road and further up the High Street. As we crossed a zebra crossing

Joe had us falling about laughing as he jumped from white stripe to black calling out in his broad Jamaican accent "Now you see me, now you don't" and "Watch it there's a car coming, I better smile at the driver!", "I have teeth like fluorescent tubing" he would brag, "Not the colour of Blue Stilton like you bloody lot" he told us.

At the slightly posher pub we managed to secure a corner for all eight of us. One would be getting the round in while the remainder drank. In this way there was no hanging about with empty glasses while the next round was being purchased. By midnight I was five-sheets to the wind, failing to keep up to my resolve not to get to pie-eyed. Then there was the sound of Big Ben chiming out the old year.

Everyone was dancing around, beer glasses sloshing around, as everyone cheered and circulated around the bar shaking hands with all the men and kissing all the women. This was right up Kev's street and he took his time and put a lot of effort in wishing all the ladies a 'Happy New Year'! He received several frowns from husbands and boyfriends who did not take too kindly to Kev's enthusiastic handling of their women.

Just after midnight I went for a much needed pee. Although the pub was very nice inside, the toilets were through a side door and up a Victorian alleyway. There were two lights in the alleyway, one outside above the side door and one above the entrance to the toilet itself. As I made my way to the toilet I heard the side door slam behind me as someone followed me out.

Unfortunately he did not make it very far and no sooner was he outside the door he began to throw up against pub wall. When I made my way back from the toilet I was very careful to avoid the pile of vomit, which looked like discarded thick vegetable soup, in the passage way, wrinkling my nose at the stench and stepping over it daintily. Back at my table I tried to warn everyone about the vomit in the alleyway. The noise in the bar was deafening and if any of them heard me, I don't think any of them were interested and cared even less. At quarter past midnight the landlord gave the large brass bell above the bar several mighty swipes with a cricket bat. "Did all pub landlords in West Bromwich have cricket bats under their bars?" I asked myself. "Last Orders! Last Orders!" He was shouting at the top of his voice trying to be heard above the din. They heard that alright and there was a mad scramble for the bar. Don graphically indicated his need to use the toilet. "Mind the spew!" I shouted as he left. He did mind the spew on his way to the toilet, but in his befuddled state, forgot all about it on his way back! He slipped on the vomit just as he got back to the side door. To try to prevent himself falling he put out his right arm.

The arm crashed through one of the small panes of glass in the door and his head broke the pane above that one. On his way back to our table he had grabbed a couple of bar towels from the bar and had wrapped them around his arm. He had a horizontal cut across his nose and his right cheekbone. He looked a terrible mess. My mother immediately flew into a blind panic.

Luckily Hallam Hospital and the A&E department was less than a mile down the road from where we were sitting. We got up and surrounded Don, taking him by the arms and easing him reluctantly out of the bar. "Come on, Don" said Dad, "lets get you down the road."

"You must be joking!" he argued, "I've still got a full pint here" and made a grab for his glass. The blood from his arm was seeping through the bar towels and beginning to drip onto the table and the floor around him. The area around us cleared of revellers as if by magic. People were standing in circle looking on. In the end my Dad, Kev and Joe had to take a hold of Don and frog marched him out of the pub and onto the high street. Don was still resisting, insisting he be allowed to finish the pint that Kev had wrenched from his hand and put on the bar on their way out. "Plenty of time" he was telling us. "Pub shuts in half an hour, the Hospital doesn't shut! Its open all night." My Dad was behind him urging him forward down the street. Kev had a hold of his injured arm and the other three lads were gathering around him, urging him to 'be sensible' and walk down to the Hospital. Muth was wailing loudly and running around the group like a headless chicken.

At that moment there was a screech of brakes. The boys in blue had arrived. I had been a fervent fan of Dixon of Dock Green as a kid and consequently had always firmly believed that every policeman always approached an incident with his hands behind his back, rocking on his feet and saying "Hello, Hello, what's going on here then?"

This illusion was dashed forever as I saw, from the corner of my eye; two of the policemen jumped from their patrol car, truncheons raised, and whistles blowing. Kev was the first to receive the policeman's enquiry with a sharp blow to the side of his head with a truncheon. He didn't even blink but turned and gave the Constable a puzzled look as if to say, "What was that for?"

One of Kev's mates was also being clobbered by another of the policeman. In answer to the whistle blowing a couple of other policeman arrived followed within the minute by a second patrol car. Muth was even more hysterical and uncontrollable. Swinging her handbag around her head began to clobber the nearest policeman about the head with it. Kev had raised his hands above his head. "Hold on, hold on!" he shouted, "What the hell you doing?" I also managed to get the attention of one of the policeman for a second or two and told him. "He slipped on some spew, we're trying to get him to A&E". He looked at me scornfully, "Go away little boy!" he snarled back at me. Kev and my Dad were still trying to calm everyone down and finally managed to achieve a semblance of order.

He found himself toe to toe, nose to nose, with one of the policeman whose right eye was beginning to discolour visibly. Kev tried to explain to the Constable what had happened. As he did so the policeman, truncheon between himself and Kev, kept leaning toward Kev provocatively, rocking slightly as if trying to push Kev backward. In the end Kev lost his patience and pushed the policeman away from him. "Will he stop bloody leaning on me!" he shouted.

Within a second the whole incident deteriorated into a full blown scrap. I, not quite as brave as the others, and attempting to stay out of trouble had backed off into a shop doorway. My Dad was arrested and shoved into the back of one of the patrol cars. They arrested my mother and did the same. Then, both of Kev's mates were arrested, they too were shoved into the back of the same patrol car. They arrested my Dad for the second time, once again pushing him into the back of the same patrol car. Then one of the policemen looked into the back. "Will one of you shut and lock the other bloody door?" he shouted, "I've arrested this lot ten times over!" One of his colleagues did so, however, there was no one in the back of the patrol car at the time.

By this time, half a dozen of the policemen had wrestled Kev to the ground and were trying desperately to get him into the car. Every time they got close he would manage to get an arm or a leg free and lash out at his tormentors.

But even under such attack Kev looked remarkable cool, calm and collected. I was pleased to see Don being led away fifty or more yards away in the direction of the hospital. Muth, Dad, Joe and someone else was with him.

Kev was sneering at those trying to get his head and shoulders into the back of the police car. "Come on" he was telling them "You can do better than that". And would then wrench an arm free and lash out with his fist. I then saw the Constable who had shut and locked the other door reach into the front of the car and from his glove compartment pulled out a large silver metal torch.

He leaned over his compatriots and shouting obscenities at Kev, began to beat Kev about the face with the torch. Until that point, I too had remained fairly calm and had been trying to persuade Kev to go quietly. I saw the torch smack Kev viciously across the bridge of the nose, which immediately released a spurt of blood. Suddenly I saw red. White lightning flashes before my eyes.

The next thing I remember was sitting calming in the back of the police car. Kev told me later that I had gone from calm to wildcat, leaping on the back of the policeman with the torch, and attempting to gauge out his eyes with my fingernails. He had managed to throw me to the ground but I was up and at 'em kicking and punching wildly at everything that looked remotely blue.

They never did manage to get Kev into the police car and six of them carried him a mile or so down the road to Black Lake and into the police station. The patrol car I was in, kerb crawled alongside, until we got there. Kev and I were handcuffed and paraded in front the half a dozen police men who all had suffered scratches, thick lips, bleeding noses, and black eyes. There was one Constable, who I recognized as the one with the torch, his whole face was particularly messy. His forehead, around his eyes and nose, and both cheeks were badly scratched and streaked with blood. He also had one of the best shiners of the lot. Another of the unfortunate policemen, who was developing two lovely black eyes, came up to Kev hurled some verbal abuse and tried to nut him in the face. However Kev had anticipated the move and lowered his head. The result being that the Constable came off worse for the attack.

A Police Sergeant appeared from somewhere and told the group of Constables to lock us up which they did. The next morning we found ourselves in front of a special Magistrate's Court, which had been traditionally held on New Years day for generations to deal with the aftermath of New Years eve. The waiting room was packed. West Bromwich had celebrated the New Year well by all accounts. Eventually Kev and I were called before the Magistrates. These comprised of three rather elderly upper class ladies, who shook their heads sadly and 'tut-tutted' as several of the more marked Constables gave their evidence.

Their evidence 'confirmed' that there were at least a dozen other men involved and several hysterical women, which must have been my Mom. Those poor constables were outnumbered by three to one. Kev and I listened in amazement at the evidence against us. It bore no relation to reality whatsoever. Kev and I both gave the same explanation when asked if we had anything to say. It was apparent that, even before we opened our mouths to speak, we would not be believed. At the end of the half hour appearance poor Kev was fined one hundred pounds, twenty pounds costs, and bound over to keep the peace for six months. I was found ten pounds. The Magistrates for breaking up a 'street riot' commended the Police Constables.

The whole incident had put a dampener on the last day of my New Years leave, as I would be leaving the next morning to return to camp. Don had nine stitches in his arm and three or four in this hand. He looked a bit of a mess as he and the rest of the family again walked me to Stone Cross. Kev, who had endured most of the police hospitality, had seemed to be none the worse for the experience, With the exception of some bruising on his arms and hands, mainly around his knuckles and a slightly swollen left eye, he was fine. Inside the lounge of the Cross Don was subject to a few curious glances from some of the other patrons. Having learned my lesson the last time I limited myself to a single pint before the family escorted me to the bus stop to see me off. They had all left their drinks on the table in the lounge so I knew that they would be going back there once I'd left.

Muth had again made me a packed lunch of beef dripping and lemon curd. However I had invested in a small thermos flask, which I thought, might also come in useful later when back at camp. The bus arrived. I suffered one of my mothers neck breaking hugs and received the usual round of handshakes and pats on the back. As I stepped aboard the Conductor sounded the bell and as before they stood waving frantically until the bus was out of sight.

I was on my way 'home'!

Chapter 18
JOURNEY SOUTH - TAKE TWO!

Just over an hour later I was back in Birmingham and making my way back to Snow Hill Station. I had had a great week, apart from New Years Night. But now, I understood, that my life had categorically and unreservedly changed forever. I realized that, whatever happened, I could never again live permanently at my parent's home. Muth had done her level best; she had changed my bed, that first day, when we got back from the Cross.

Sadly I didn't sleep that well during my leave, unless it was alcohol induced, the bed was full of lumps and bumps, smelt musty, dusty an damp. I had to try to sleep close to the edge of the bed because, near the centre of the mattress I could feel a hard ring of metal as one of the springs attempted to burst through an old blanket that had been strategically placed over it. I could almost taste the mould that grew on the damp age old wallpaper in almost every corner of every room of the pre-war house.   For the first time since I had first left home, I could feel the effects of all this on my health, particularly on my chest. I hadn't had an asthma attack since I had left home, but during my leave, I came close to it.

Now my two brothers, Kev and Don, were well known all over Birmingham, West Bromwich, Smethwick, Wednesbury, Walsall, Tipton. In fact just about everywhere. The ordinary townsfolk looked on them as a sort of Robin Hood Duo, even though they sometimes forgot who the poor were.

When they had money they were generous, perhaps over generous, to friends and colleagues and after a pint or two even to total strangers! I looked upon them as a pair of 'Del Boys' who always believed that tomorrow they would make it rich. If I had not joined the Army when I did I am quite convinced I would have finished up as their 'Rodney'.

They were both now in there early twenties. They had never had a proper job. When they left school, just as I had found, work was pretty hard to come by. Kev and Don started off earning their pocket money on the council tips, looking for wiring and scrap metals, to take to the tat-man. If they had a good day they could weigh in a good fivers worth of scrap, but those days were few and far between. They were forever being chased off the council tip by the day time watchmen whose job it was to keep tatters like Kev and Don off the tip. At night and at weekends it was a different story. There was no watchman after about five o'clock or at the weekends. They had no trouble scaling the gates or fences that surrounded the tip.

They progressed from tatting to demolitions. They would check the local paper, 'the Express and Star' almost daily to read the 'Public Notices'. The various town councils published in their notices those buildings and houses that were due to be demolished. There was a lot of demolition work going on at that time. Kev and Don, with a couple of mates if needed, would go to the demolition site well before those who had been contracted to carry out the work.

In this way they could remove everything of value such as the roof tiles, timbers, flooring, piping and wiring, in fact anything that they could sell on, before the contractors arrived. Because of their profession they had more than several run ins with the local constabulary. Most of the local constabulary knew them by sight and many were 'mates' off duty!

Of course Big Ears knew them well from their school days and would keep a, not unfriendly, look out for them. He would warn them to steer clear of his patch and they generally did so, preferring to carry out their occupation some distance from home. They did prosper. Kev had an 'unofficial' yard over Tipton way, where he stored all the timber, roof tiles and the like and between them they had managed to get their hands on an old Bedford lorry they used to transport their products from site to yard. You could understand then why it was the local constabulary maintained an interest in their whereabouts and what they were up to.

One particular weekend, Don, having had a successful morning stripping a certain house of anything of value, retired to a local pub and celebrated with half a dozen or more pints. He still had a fair bit of lead sheeting he needed to get rid of. So he decided to visit a local tat-man on his way home. Unfortunately it was getting a little late, it was dark, and it was drizzling a little. Don found an old pram on the site, which, although it had only three wheels, would help him transport the lead to his tat-man friend.

However, strolling along West Bromwich High Street, pushing a three wheeled pram, caught the eye of a suspicious policeman. The end result was Don was arrested and his lead confiscated. All was not lost. During the night Don managed to get out through the tiny lift up window of his cell and climbed out and on to the roof of the old Victorian Police Station. Don had not been idle on the roof of the Police Station. He found that the roof had a large amount of lead around the bases of the half a dozen or so chimney stacks, along the apex of the roof and around the attic windows. He decided to take full advantage of his predicament and stripped the Police Station roof of lead, finishing up with more than what they had originally confiscated from him. He threw the lead down into the rather overgrown gardens at the rear of the Station. They discovered him missing early the next morning. While they carried out a search of the local area, Don quietly continued removing any last bits of lead he could find. He recruited Kev to help him recover this little nest egg a couple of weeks later when the hoo-ha had died down.

At Snow Hill station I took stock, I still had close to ten pounds left, and was pleased with that. I sat on a bench and taking out Muth's Beef Dripping sandwich, began to eat. It was OK, don't get me wrong, but even this erstwhile favourite of mine had somehow lost its appeal. The lemon curd sandwiches, I'm sorry to admit, went straight to the pigeons. I enjoyed the tea though, still nice and hot, from my new thermos flask. While strolling around waiting for my train I finished up in the bookshop and bought two 'J T Edson' cowboy books.

It was while waiting to pay for these that I heard the announcement that my train was due in ten minutes. Having slipped the books into my little suitcase I took out my wallet to get my ticket ready before moving through the small barrier, which led on to the platform. I searched every fold of the wallet two or three times. The ticket wasn't there. Panic!

In the vain hope of finding my ticket I retraced my steps and carried out a search around the bench I had been sitting at earlier. Finally, in desperation, I approached the ticket barrier and spoke to the porter there. "Sorry mate!" he told me, "no ticket, no train"

"What am I going to do?" I asked him, "I haven't enough cash for another ticket!"

"Go see the police, they can give you a replacement rail warrant", he told me.

"But I'll miss my train", I moaned.

"Mail train in a hour!" he said. "If you hurry you should make it!"

"Where is the Police Station?" I asked in frustration.

"Out the Station, bear right, few hundred yards down the street".

"Thanks!" I groaned despondently.

"Don't mention it!" he replied.

So off I went. "I'm bloody plagued with bad luck," I told myself, "I'm jinxed".

A quarter of an hour later I found the Police Station and went in. They were busy.

"'Scuse me Sgt!" I called, waving my hand over several other individuals seeking attention.

"Lost my train ticket, I need a Train Warrant",

"You'll have to wait!" the policeman shouted back.

"My train is in an hour," I shouted back.

"Tough titty" the police called back.

"Wait your turn," someone said from behind me.

"Sorry?" I asked turning around.

"Lost my ticket to Portsmouth!" he informed me. He put his hand out. "Seaman 'Somebody', mate". I shook his hand.

"Royal Engineers" I told him, "Where did you loose your ticket" I asked him.

"If I knew where I lost my ticket, it wouldn't be lost now would it!" he answered.

"Silly question" I admitted. "What time's your train?"

"I'll have to get the mail train to London, now" he said, "That's if these lot will get their finger out!" The sailor stood up and approached the desk once more.

"Come on Constable" he called "give us a break!"

The Constable gave an irritated sigh of annoyance and made his way over to a desk. The sailor was called to a desk at the other side of the room, they chatted some, and the sailor presented his ID Card. Five minutes later he got up, walking past me he said "I'd wait for you, but don't want to risk missing the train" and he disappeared out of the door.

"You!" beckoned the policeman at the desk, and indicating the chair the sailor had so recently vacated.

The policeman continued to write in his report book for a moment or two before looking up at me.

"Name?" he asked, pen poised.

"Houghton".

"Rank?"

"Sapper".

"Number" he asked again, still without looking up.

I gave my number. "Unit"

"No 1 Training Regiment, Royal Engineers".

The policeman had stopped writing. He looked at me again, rubbing his chin. "Houghton, Hmmmm, Houghton, where you from boy?" he asked.

"Wednesbury! I told him. "Know the name!" he said to himself quietly, "Houghton".

I sat there, not having a clue what the policeman was on about. The Constable walked over to some of his colleagues and had a little muted conversation, nodding in my direction as he did so. A minute or two later he returned bringing a Police Sgt with him to the desk I was sitting at. They both looked at me with undisguised interest. The Sgt Sat down at the desk the Constable had vacated.

"Houghton?" the Police Sergeant asked.

"Yes" I replied. "You know a Kev and a Don Houghton by any chance?"

"My brothers" I confirmed. They both leaned across the desk towards me. "Seen them lately?" asked the Sergeant. "Saw me off at the bus stop" I told them.

"Where?" the Sergeant asked leaning even closer.

"We had a farewell drink in the Navigation" I told them, the Navigation being several miles from the Cross at the opposite end of the Friar Park estate.

The Police Sergeant almost ran back to his desk and started to chat to people on his radio. I could almost hear him saying "Calling all cars, calling all cars" in true Dixon of Dock Green fashion. The policeman I had talked to filled out my replacement rail warrant in record time and thrust it into my hand. "On your way, lad" he told me.

Back at Snow Hill Station I managed to catch the mail train with just seconds to spare. No sooner had I slammed the door of the train on the first carriage I came to, the guard on the train blew his whistle, waved his green flag and off we went. Finding an empty carriage I settled down in the corner, took out my J T Edson cowboy book 'Edge', and began to read. I must have dozed off at some point. What woke me was the announcement that we would shortly be arriving at Watford Junction. I looked at my watch. I had had a good sleep; just over two hours had passed since I boarded the train.

I took out my flask and poured myself a cup of tea, not as hot, but still nice. Having drunk my tea I got up and moved into the corridor of the train and waited there for the last half hour of my journey into London. I had learned from the mistakes I had made on my first trip on the underground and arrived at Victoria station just half an hour after my arrival at London Euston, well in time to catch the train to Aldershot that I had missed by about ten minutes the first time I journeyed south.

At Cove, it was, as before, dark and Station closed. I walked straight through and after a brief look around found the number of a local taxi firm in a phone box. I had no intention of walking to the Camp as I had done the first time. The taxi firm informed me that the fare would be five shillings, plus a shilling, for late evening. Within half an hour of my arrival at Cove the taxi pulled up outside the gates of Southwood Camp. I generously gave the taxi driver seven shillings, a shilling tip, which he accepted with a grunt.

I walked into camp and up to the window at the Guard Room to report my return. To my utter consternation I was promptly arrested!

"What have I done?" I asked as the Cpl who escorted me unceremoniously into a cell.

"You tell me" he replied with indifference, "All I got is a note that you are to be detained on return to camp," he said. They didn't even allow me one of their cheese sandwiches or a cup of tea. Locked in my cell I pulled a blanket overhead, and fully clothed, eventually managed to fall to sleep.

At about eight o'clock the next morning the Sgt Major, who had been present when I had been charged with assaulting the Provost Sgt, collected me from the Guard Room and escorted me to the Squadron Office. He informed me that I was to be charged with "Committing a Civil Offence contrary to Section 70 of the Army Act 1955 in that I, in West Bromwich, on the 1 January, did assault PC 'Bigfoot' during the execution of his duties" "Bloody 'ell" I thought to myself "News travels fast!" A few minutes later I was pounding the boards in front of the same Major that had fined me for beating the Provost Sgt and for loosing the Bren Gun. However, on this occasion, he was quite informal. Having read the charges to me, he warned me that this was a very serious offence, and that I better have good mitigating circumstances, whatever that meant! I took my time and explained about Don slipping on the vomit, that he had put his arm and face through the door window, and that my Dad, myself, my brother Kev and several others had attempted to persuade him to come with us to the hospital.

I also, without malice, and as factual as I could, explained what had happened when the police had arrived. That they had not even tried to ascertain what had happened or taken the time to even question anyone. That it was they, the police and not us, which were the cause of the fracas.

The Major listened intently to what I had to say. If only the Magistrates had paid half as much attention, I thought to myself, things might have turned out very differently. I was in the Major's Office for a good hour. He left me sitting there for a while, while he mulled things over. Coming to a decision he told me, "I am sorry, Houghton, but I have no alternative, this offence will be recorded on your service records" he told me.

"Yes, Sir" I replied.

"But" he went on "I do not intend to impose any other penalty on you".

"Thank you, Sir" I replied.

"But I must warn you, Houghton" he continued "Should there be a repeat of such behaviour, I will have no alternative but to recommend that you be discharged from the Army as 'Services No Longer Required', do you understand?"

"Yes, Sir".

"March him out Sgt Major!" with that I was marched out of the Major's Office and told to report for duty.

Back at Spider 10, I immediately felt at home, the room smelt of polish, bleach, brasso and fresh Blanco! Only about half a dozen were back, the others still had plenty of time, until five p.m. to report back at the Guard Room.

Peter was not back yet, neither Heaton nor Jock. Smith was though, and I invited him to the NAAFI for a bite to eat and a quick game of pool, which we did. I took the opportunity to spend a penny and was astounded to find I was only a pound or two under eight and a half stone. Must have been all the beer I had drunk during my weeks leave. Peter turned up at about three o'clock and I told him what at happened during the early hours of New Years Day and what had happened on my return. He was a little indignant, on my behalf, saying one should not be tried twice for the same offence. He also told me that the week before we completed out training in March he had to report to the Royal Military Academy, Sandhurst, to commence his Officer Training, but that he would return for, and be part of, our Pass Out Parade. He had had a row with his father by all accounts, who wanted him to follow in his footsteps and join the Worcester and Sherwood Foresters. Peter had insisted that he would remain in the Royal Engineers. Good for him!

The next morning, our first morning back in training, there was a notice on the Troop Notice Board asking for people to put in their preferences for posting on completion of their training in March. Of course it was a foregone conclusion that not everyone would get where they asked for. Most put in for postings to such as Malaya, Singapore, Hong Kong and other such exotic places. I considered putting in for Jamie's unit, but instantly dismissed the idea. I did not think he would like his little brother being around watching his every move. I certainly didn't want be in his shadow either. In the end I wrote 'Not UK'.

I was happy to be posted anywhere outside of the UK and I left it at that. Heaton followed suit informing me that he would be more than happy to get a posting to Germany. Peter left his preference blank, annotating the list 'Sandhurst'. Little did he or I know that seven months later we were to meet again?

Also, displayed on the Troop Notice Board was an announcement that the Army Boxing Finals would be held in Aldershot during the second weekend of January. It would be the Royal Engineers versus the Royal Artillery. Volunteers were required to act as 'Ushers' and 'Waiters'. I didn't fancy the idea of 'ushering' whatever that entailed, but the opportunity to wait on was very appealing. I put my name down in the hope I could get a position as a waiter, after all, I had experience!

Our first four days back in training, the Tuesday until Friday, we underwent a series of revision on drill, two PT lessons a day, a run or the gymnasium in the morning and the assault course in the afternoon. A lot of time was being spent measuring us up for our No 2 Dress Uniforms that had to be tailor made. We would not get our new No 2 Dress Uniforms until late February or early March, but in time for our Pass Out parade. Over the next two weeks we spent a lot of time on Hawley Lake using aluminum 'Combat Support Boats, which was brilliant. During this waterborne training I imagined myself carrying out landings in Normandy, storming Hitler's 'Fortress Europe', or charging up sandy beaches to take on hoards of fanatical Japanese. It was great fun.

We were also trained on building and dismantling the 'Heavy Ferry', which could ferry up to nine fully laden 10 ton lorries or six tanks at a time across the water. The engines were huge. I was told they cost up to ten thousand pounds each! Our main problem was steering the damn thing. Those manning the rear two engines had to steer in the opposite direction to the two front ones when turning, it was very confusing.

We came close to running the thing aground on more than one occasion, much to the aggravation of poor Sgt Steel, who ended up nearly pulling his hair out in sheer frustration. However by the end of the fortnight we could steer the Heavy Ferry in a reasonably straight line from A to B.

Towards the end of that fortnight we learned that Sgt Steel was to be on leave for three weeks from the Friday of the following week. Apparently his wife was due to give birth to twins. We found this highly amusing, not able to visualize just how Mrs. Steel found herself in this state. It was like trying imagining how our Mothers had got into that condition.

Over the next week poor Sgt Steel had to put up with an unceasing amount of innuendos whenever he spoke to us or came within earshot. There was a particularly obnoxious rugby song, which we would hum to ourselves whenever he walked by or entered the room.

Part of it went something like . . .

> . . . *So they built a Prick of Steel*
> *Driven by a bloody great wheel*
> *A hum titty bum titty bum titty bum*
> *A hum titty bum titty bum titty bum*

We had changed the word 'of' in the song to ' for' you get the picture! Poor old Sgt Steel. But he took it with great deal of tolerance. "They'll get over it!" I heard him tell one of the Cpl's "the novelty will soon wear off!" We decided to have a whip round for the Steel twins and gave it him on Friday morning before he departed on leave. Most of us put a couple of bob in the pot, Peter, rather nonchalantly dropped in a ten-shilling note.

From all of the rooms we collected about eleven pounds something. We did not know, of course, what sex the children would be, and there was much discussion and dispute about what should we do with the money. In the end Peter suggested we buy two lots of premium bonds, five pounds per child, as an investment for their future. With the change we could buy a bunch of flowers for Mrs. Steel.

Come the Friday morning Peter and I were elected to do the honours. On parade I had to hide the flowers behind my back when Sgt Steel emerged to take us on our PT session.

"Attention!" he commended. We all came smartly to attention.

"By the Left, Left Turn" he bellowed. We all did a smart Right Turn!

For a second he doubted himself. He looked as if he was unsure whether he had ordered a left turn or a right turn. He must have given us the benefit of the doubt. We were all now facing the wrong way. .

"Ayyy bout, Turn! He bellowed. We all did a second smart Right Turn.

Sgt Steel couldn't believe his senses, what the hell were we doing. It then became obvious. Because by turning right the second time we now all had our backs to him. I stood in the centre of the back row revealing the large bunch of flowers. The poor man became speechless. "Ayyy bout, Turn" Peter called out, rather professionally I thought. Would make a good officer! We were now back in our original position facing Sgt Steel. He looked very embarrassed and not sure what to do next. Peter and I stepped forward as one. I handed Sgt Steel the flowers singing out in a loud voice.

These are for your Mrs. Steel!
Ah hum, A hum
These are for your Mrs. Steel!
From all the lads in your dear team!
A hum titty bum titty bum titty bum
A hum titty bum titty bum titty bum

The whole parade joined in. There were a number of catcalls and whistles during which Peter gave Sgt Steel the Congratulations Card that contained the two lots of five pound premium bonds. Sgt Steel rubbed his nose, scratched his head and handed the flowers and the card to a conveniently placed Cpl.

"Right you miserable lot, you poor excuse for manhood, I'll teach you to take the piss out of me!" There followed one of the hardest forced marches we had had. I am sure we did a good mile more than we should have done. Almost all of the way there and back all Sgt Steel could hear was

'A hum titty bum titty bum, titty bum!
A hum titty bum titty bum titty bum!'

227

Chapter 19
THE MIGHTY, THE ONE AND ONLY, ITS WAM BAM HOUGHTON!!

Saturday morning we found a rather nice note pinned to the Troop Notice Board. It was not a hand we recognized, it certainly was not Sgt Steels illegible scrawl. The note, in a delicate handwriting, thanked us all for the most wonderful flowers and the thoughtful and delightful gifts to our yet unborn children. It was a rather delightful note from Mrs. Steel. We all felt rather good after reading it.

At eleven o'clock we boarded a three ton truck to take us to Aldershot for the Army Boxing Championship. I still did not know whether I would be an usher or a waiter but would, I concluded, find out in due course.

I managed to secure a seat next to the tailgate of the lorry and took great pleasure, as we drove through the town, in admiring the ladies as they went about their Saturday shopping. There were the inevitable cat calls and whistles as we drove through at those young ladies deemed worthy of the compliment.

Some ignored us but most smiled and gave us a little wave. It was very nice. On arrival in Aldershot we were paraded in front of the large gymnasium and addressed by the RSM, the Regimental Sergeant Major, who, lifting his gleaming pace stick to shoulder height shouted. "Those to the left, report to Sgt Some-body-or-other as Ushers".

The left half of the squad broke away and moved across to stand next to the indicated Sgt. "Those to the right report to Sgt 'Someone-Else' as Waiters". "Damn" I said to myself, annoyed, "Another two paces to the left and I'd be a waiter!" Our Sgt escorted us into the Gymnasium and positioned us in two's and three's at key points close to entrances and aisles to direct people where to sit.

"Red tickets, WO's and Sgts over there, Blue tickets, Junior NCOs this side, Yellow tickets, soldiers, down that side" we were told.

"What about the Officers?" I asked hopefully.

"They don't need tickets lad", he replied, they will walk over from the Officer's Mess when everyone else is in and seated".

"No chance then!" I moaned to myself, the waiters are obviously over the Officer's Mess.

I found myself at the Red Ticket entrance, which I was pleased to note, was adjacent to the dressing rooms. This is where all the action was! I would be seeing the boxers coming out and returning after their fights. My imagination took flight and I imagined myself training a top boxer.

"My Lords, Ladies and Gentlemen" I whispered to myself. I subconsciously hopped about, from one foot to the other, fists raised in a classic boxers pose! Ready to take on Mohammed Ali.

"Stop day dreaming lad" the RSM screamed at me. I hadn't even heard him approach. "And pay attention to your ushering!" "Yes, Sir".

"I ain't ushered anybody yet" I thought to myself, "they all seem to know where they are going without an ush!"

Everyone, except the Officers were in and sitting about. There was a loud hubbub of din and chatter, which together with the scraping chairs, was rather deafening. Looking around I noted that the Royal Engineers had provided a goodly number of spectators. More than the Artillery I thought. I wondered if Jamie was here. I could not see their faces from the back so it was no use trying to find out.

Out of the corner of my eye I saw one of the entrances open and a huge stream of Officers, resplendent in the Mess Uniforms, and their ladies, all dressed in evening gowns, make a grand entrance. The noise lessened. When the last of the Officers and their Ladies had taken their seats there was a rumble of drums. The Royal Engineer Band was here! I hadn't noticed them on the far side of the boxing ring. They played the first verse of 'God Save the Queen' and we all stood to attention. The anthem over we sat down and the finals were under way.

First up were the Heavyweights. The swing doors behind me flew open and this massive bloke, built like an ox and flanked by two corner men, came hopping and skipping down the aisle, shadow boxing to left and right as he went.

"Anyone mad enough to get in the ring with him" I thought to myself. "Needs their heads looking at!" A minute later the doors flew open a second time. I didn't think it possible, this man seemed even bigger! He too huffed and puffed and boxed his way down to the ring.

I could tell that this one was the Royal Engineer by his blue and maroon shorts and the Corps badge on the left leg. I started hopping about again in sheer excitement; you could cut the atmosphere with a knife.

The announcer did his bit, very well I thought, using terms such as "Fearsome Fred" and "Theodore the Thug!" I was convinced he was making up the names as he went along. When the first bell sounded I was bursting with exhilaration and anticipation. The fight went the full three rounds, the whole time, I found myself jumping up and down, using arms and fists as if to help our man beat his opponent senseless. I knew our man had won. I was utterly convinced. When the referee raised the Artilleryman's arm I cried out in dismay. Cupping my hands around my mouth I let out a huge 'boo'. Several of those seated in front of me turned around giving me a vicious look. They were all Artillerymen. A Sgt at the end of the row nearest me got up and came towards me. "One more sound out of you my lad" he growled at me "And you'll get this!" pushing his fist to with a millimetre of my nose.

Three more fights followed in quick succession, our chap's won two of them, one by a knockout. I heard the swing doors behind me open. I didn't look round, I knew it would be a minute or two before the next boxer appeared. Suddenly I was grabbed by the back of my neck and pulled backward. I twisted around to see my assailant. It was one of the corner men I had seen earlier. He was a Royal Engineer the Corps badge visible on his vest.

He looked at my cap badge. "You'll do!" he declared and dragged me by the scruff of the neck through the swing doors and down the corridor.

"I'll do what?" I asked him several times. I found myself in the dressing room with a young man, in shorts and vest, nursing his wrist.

"Get your kit off" the trainer told the lad. Then turning to me said "You too".

"Me?"

"Yes, You!"

"What for?" I asked. A horrible realization was beginning to filter into my terrified brain.

"Hurt his wrist" the trainer told me. I knew something terrible was about to happen to me.

"Hurry up, get a move on" he shouted at me. I began to undress, objecting profusely as each item of clothing hit the floor.

"I can't box, I don't know how to box, I have never boxed in my life" I whined at him.

"Listen to me" the trainer explained. "Winner gets two points, loser gets one point, if there is a no show, we don't get any points, understand?"

"No, I don't want to fight anyone!"

"That one point might be the difference between winning the tournament or loosing!" he shouted "And you are going to get that one point".

The injured lad had changed into a tracksuit and left to watch the bouts.

"Listen to me" the trainer, told me "Just keep moving, hop about a lot, and keep looking your opponent straight in the eye, to phsyc him out".

"What him out?" I asked. He patted me on the shoulder, "just dance about a bit, jab jab jab, if your opponent hits you, go down!"

"Go down?" I repeated lamely. "Hit the canvas" he confirmed "Hey presto, one point to us".

The trainer sat me down and was rubbing my arms and legs as if I was the real boxer.

"Keep ducking and diving, jab jab jab, watch his right hand, keep moving," he was telling me. All the time he was bandaging my hands with white tape and before I realized what he was doing my gloves were on. They weighed a ton. How was I supposed to hit anyone with these? I just sat there and tried very hard not to have a humiliating accident in a pair of Corps Boxer Shorts. Every time I heard the crowd roar or the swing doors open I had to resist the burning compulsion to make a run for it. The trainer must have been reading my mind because he never let go of my wrists the whole time he chattered away. I hadn't the slightest idea about what he was saying to me. The door to the dressing room opened. A head appeared briefly. "Next" it said. I almost wet myself.

Next thing I knew I was being trundled, if not frog marched, out of the dressing room down the corridor and out into the gymnasium. There was a huge roar as I emerged.

"Keep your arms up, box!" the trainer growled at me. I tried very hard to prance about as I had watched previous boxers do and began flinging my arms out left and right in a futile imitation of someone who knows what he's doing. By the time I got down to ringside my arms were aching from the oversized boxing gloves. At the side of the ring the trainer turned me to face him.

"Now remember, just keep moving, keep one eye on his right hand, and keep jabbing away, God knows" he said, "You might drop lucky".

"You're totally insane," I told him, "I am going to hit that canvas the first chance I get".

"Yeah" he scoffed "Make sure you wait until after the bell has gone won't you".

He turned me to face the ring, with an affectionate pat on the bum; he hoisted me into the ring. He followed me in and sat me on the stool.

"Don't drop your eyes or look away," he instructed "Just keep looking him straight in the eye"

"OK" I replied.

"And for Christ sake don't smile at him!"

"I won't".

The announcer entered the ring and took up his position centre stage. "My Lords, Ladies and Gentlemen" he boomed. "Do your best lad" the trainer whispered, "that's all I ask" so saying he pushed me into the ring. I stood next to the announcer. "May I present to you this afternoon, in the blue corner" . "That's not me," I said to myself.

"Lightning Lad Gunner Larry Holmes" he continued. There was a roar of approval from the Artillery side of the Gymnasium. Many of them getting to their feet and whistling and jabbing the air with their fists.

"And in the Red Corner". "Oh Shit!" I said aloud "May I present to you the one and only!"

"And never again" I said to myself.

"The one and only Wam Bam Houghton!" There was an even bigger roar, I looked around nervously and to my amazement found that most of the Engineers were on their feet cheering.

"Bloody 'ell" I thought, and they don't even know me from Adam. "Cave his head in Wam Bam," someone close to the ring shouted. "Wam Bam, Wam Bam" they chanted at me. I couldn't believe my ears, where the hell did they get that from? "I've been stitched up" I thought, "Some bugger has done me up like a kipper!"

The announcer backed off, handed his microphone to his assistant, and bowed out of the ring. The referee stepped forward and taking our hands turned us to face each other. "I want a clean fight, break when I tell you," Without realizing it I shuffled a little closer to my opponent, almost nose to nose, I stared him right in the eye. He is as scared as I am I realized. "Defend yourselves at all times" the referee concluded. He backed away a few feet. My opponent and I backed off towards our respective corners. "Keep moving, jab jab jab," my trainer screamed at me. 'Ding! Ding!' Round One, I heard over the speakers.

Lightning Larry came out of his corner like a bullet. Hands up covering his face. "Oh yeah! I whispered to myself. "Keep my hands up, keep moving" I found myself prancing and ducking around the ring with Lightning Larry following closely. I was talking to myself the whole time. Partly out of utter terror, partly to remind myself what to do. Lightning Larry punched me two or three times. "Hmmm" I remember thinking, "Doesn't hurt that much with these gloves on!" We must have circled and pranced around for half the round, a full minute and a half, when I found myself very close to my own corner.

"You are supposed to hit the bloody man back," the trained screamed at the top of his voice.

"Jab jab jab" then "For Christ sake, hit him"

We danced around a bit more; I took another two or three punches. Suddenly, for the first time since the fight began, I looked up and stared Lightning Larry in the eye. From nowhere I produced a left hook that he must have seen coming from half a mile away. It caught him squarely on the chin.

He hit the canvas as if I had hit him with a twelve pound sledgehammer. I knew that it was impossible for me to have hit him that hard. Was it possible that Lightning Larry was in the ring just to make sure of one point, as I was?

The Royal Engineer audience went wild, jumping to their feet, screaming Wam Bam! Wam Bam! The referee ordered me to a neutral corner. As I turned I saw Lightning Larry roll onto his back. His eyes shut, he was licking his lips. There was the tiniest, smallest possible speck of blood you could possibly imagine. But Lightning Larry could taste it. I suddenly heard the referee counting, "six, seven, eight, nine, and out!" he shouted waving his arms across the fallen man. He reached over and raised my right arm. I raised my left automatically in salute. The roar was deafening. I jumped up and down on the spot and spun around arms raised.

The next thing I knew I was being swamped by the trainers, towel around my shoulders.

"Well done, magnificent left hook that!" he praised.

"Really?" I replied, "It hardly touched him".

"Rubbish" they said, "That was a cracker".

I enjoyed the clamour and cheers as I was led away back to the dressing room.

Once there the trainer insisted I had the makings of a flyweight boxer, "Would I like that?" he asked me.

"Like a hole in the head" I told him "And if anyone thinks they will get me in the ring again, they have another thing coming". I started to remove my shorts to get changed back into my uniform.

"Can't get changed yet, lad," he told me, "You have to wait for the presentations at the end".

"What presentations? I asked foolishly.

"You might get two" he informed me, "One for winning the flyweight division, and hopefully, if we're lucky, one for being part of the winning team."

Someone from somewhere produced a large mug of hot sweet tea. I sat there and sipped it while I waited for this nightmare to end.

The Royal Engineers won, in the end, by three bouts. I found myself being led, together with seven other boxers, back into the ring. None of my boxers new me of course, and gave me inquisitive stares. However, they all congratulated me on my superb win. "Utter poppycock" I thought to myself. One of the senior officers climbed into the ring and a table covered with the Royal Engineer Flag was hoisted in after him. He went along the line dishing out a pair of medallions to each of the boxers. I was last in line, being the flyweight. He stood in front of me, he was tall, and I looked up. "Christ almighty, it was the Colonel I had waited on in his home before Christmas". I told myself.

"Well, well, well, Houghton, you seem to pop up in the strangest of places".

"You're telling me!" I replied.

"Pardon?"

"I mean, Yes, Sir".

"How did you get into the Corps Boxing Team? You haven't been in the Army five minutes"

"It's a long story" I replied.

"I bet it is" he said "But congratulations, magnificent fight, you have done the Corps proud".

"Thank you, Sir" he shook my hand. He leaned forward slightly.

"Mars" he whispered "God of War eh?" referring to our previous meeting.

With that he turned about and climbed out of the ring.

There was another resounding cheer as we all filed out of the ring back to the dressing room.

Half an hour later, showered and changed back into uniform I left the gymnasium to find the three ton truck waiting to take me back to camp. All the lads were aboard and as I emerged from the gymnasium they gave me a cheer. On the way back I dispelled their illusions that I was a reincarnation of Rocky Marciano. I explained what had happened and how I had finished up in the ring. They were understandably incredulous. Finally, I admitted to them that I thought the other chap had also been told to take a dive. They poo-pooed that idea telling me I had won fair and square.

I still wonder, even today, about that left uppercut!

Chapter 20
THE END OF THE BEGINNING

Just about a week after my ordeal in the ring I received a letter, no more than a note, from my brother Jamie. The note simply said. "I was five rows back, watched your fight, Well done, Wam Bam! Luv Jamie". So Jamie had been there. I found out later that a thirty-six seater coach had come up from 22 Engineer Regiment to support the Engineer Team. Always on the lookout of ways and means to avoid the humdrum routine of service life in barracks, Jamie had volunteered to attend. He had been absolutely gob smacked to see me appear in the ring, let alone win!

Sgt Steel arrived at the Troop Office one morning and pinned another nice note from his better half together with a large photograph of his two or three week or old twins. A girl and a boy, Adam and Hillary.

The photograph remained on the board for a day or two before it was stolen. We were put out more than a little by its disappearance. Sgt Steel tried to make out that its disappearance was a trivial matter. We knew Sgt Steel well and we knew that its disappearance would have hurt his feelings. The last couple of weeks of February and early March were all 'practice makes perfect'. We practiced everything, one, twice, three-times. We revised our demolitions, our mine warfare, our trench digging, our drill and rifle drill, our bridging, everything. Over and over.

From the second week of March our drill began to take a more prominent roll as we practiced and rehearsed for our final pass out parade on 22 March. On the first Monday in March we were issued our first of two, No 2 Dress uniforms complete with No 1 Dress Hat et al. These had to be pressed immaculately for our Pass Out Parade and we had to endure innumerable 'best kit inspections' until Lt Mortimer and Sgt Steel were totally satisfied with our turnout.

During the first week of March the postings were displayed on the Troop Notice Board. No sooner had the list been pinned up on the board, the word was out, and a throng of eager men were pushing, shoving and elbowing there way through the throng, in their eagerness to locate their names and the units to which they were to be posted. Some cheered, many groaned, two thirds of us were to be posted to UK units. There was only one fortunate lad posted to what one might consider an exotic posting, and that was Heaton. He was posted to 62 (NE) Support Squadron in Cyprus. Two places below his, I found my name, Osnabruck, Germany. "That will do me nicely," I thought to myself.

I could not wait to find out where Osnabruck was using Peter's atlas.

As the end of our training drew near spirits were high. In the early hours of one morning we crept silently into room two, in our stocking feet. One or two of the occupants woke up, but seeing what we were about, did not raise the alarm.

We tied four lengths of rope on each corner of the 'bullies' bed, passed the ends over the cross beams in the ceiling, gently hoisted up so that his bed was roughly six feet from the ground. According to some of the lads in room two, when the Training Cpl came in at reveille a few hours later, he just stopped and stared at the bed hanging from the ceiling. Then hit the bed with his stick shouting "Up and at em". The bully rolled from his bed, realizing too late that the floor had disappeared, hit the floor with a thump. His comrades where highly amused and very pleased at his downfall.

Many of us in room one had dispensed with pyjamas. For one thing the weather was warming up and two, it was one less item of military clothing that had to be washed, pressed, folded and placed onto the correct shelf in your locker, for inspection. Room two did not take long to exact their revenge upon us. As I have said many times before, never take the first bed in a barrack room, because, as usual, mine was the first bed they came to.

I always slept well, and usually I could sleep through anything, as often being the last one out of bed in the mornings proved. My roommates often referred to me as 'The Mole' because normally, once in bed, I would pull the sheets and blankets over my head to block out any light. I think it also stemmed from the fact that at home, the house was so cold and damp; it was the easiest way to keep warm on chilly nights.

Room two crept into my room, at about three a.m., they told me later. They lifted up my bed and carried me out of the room, down the corridor, and out onto the parade ground. There they left me, a note cellotaped to the end of my bed which read 'Wam Bam the Windowlene Man' accompanied by a crude drawing of an Officer covered all down the front with pink fluid.

I do remember, as I was slowly regained my awareness, that there was a terrible draft in the room. Peter was famed for opening the window beside his bed at every opportunity. Usually within five minutes, one or other of us pulled it shut again. "Shut the bloody window, Peter" I moaned from deep down in my bed. "It's bloody freezing".

There was no answer. I suddenly thought "'Ello, they're awfully quiet this morning!" It was when I was just picking up the courage to poke my head out when someone boomed out, close to where my head was under the blankets.

"What the 'ell are you doing on my Parade Ground laddie?"

"Parade Ground?" His shout made me jump a mile; frightened out of my wits I threw back the blankets. The big Sgt with the red sash was standing over me grinning.

"You like sleeping in the big outdoors?" he asked.

"No, Sgt" I stammered.

"Up" he shouted, giving me a poke with his stick. "And stand to attention when I'm talking to you". I swiveled my feet to the ground wrapping the sheet around my middle.

"I can't Sgt," I pleaded.

"Up I said" he shouted leaning forward so that we were almost nose to nose.

"Got no pyjamas on" I groaned at him. I could see people stopping to stare, enjoying the situation, and wondering about the outcome. More than a few were ladies on their way to their respective secretarial, typing, cleaning, and washing up work places.

"You won't frighten me with anything you have got", you excuse of a man, then, waving his pace stick around him, nor any one else for that matter!"

I climbed off the bed, still trying to hide my vital statistics with my blankets. Practically every one from Spider 10 had also emerged to watch. The Sgt with the red sash leaned forward, picked up a pillow and threw it at me.

"Here you are lad!" he said, "Now go and get dressed, and if that bed is not removed from my Parade Ground in five minutes, I will rip your arms off and beat you with the soggy ends".

I grabbed the pillow, holding it strategically, a few inches below my belly button, and with right hand behind me in a vain attempt to cover my rear; I scurried back to my room.

"You lot!" the Sgt bellowed as I ran, indicating those from Spider 10, "Get this 'effing bed off my Parade Ground now!"

Peter and several others ran to retrieve my bed.

That same day I had another run in with our illustrious Sgt with the red sash. Peter and I, with several others were hurrying to the cookhouse for our lunch when we ran in to him again.

He was driving a Landrover, but this Landrover had been stripped down, no canvas back, and the top halves of the doors removed. It resembled a Jeep. In fact at first, we all thought it was a Jeep. He pulled up at the side of the road and, as is his wont, gave us a hard time about not keeping in step properly. I had to open my big mouth didn't I? In an effort to get on his good side I said.

"I like your Jeep, Sgt!" He was out, beside me, screaming in my right ear, quicker that you can say Jack Robinson.

"What did you call it?"

"A Jeep, Sgt" "An 'effin Jeep?" He liked his colourful language this one did. I hardly ever heard Sgt Steel use such language.

"This is a Landrover" he balled at me.

"Sorry, Sgt" I grimaced, "But it looks like a Jeep!"

"It looks nothing like an 'effin Jeep, you moron". Peter and the others were standing around looking sympathetic. We were within yards of the cookhouse. In fact I could see faces appear at the cookhouse window as people's curiosity got the better of them. The Sgt beckoned me to his 'Jeep'.

"Up" he commanded. Tapping the bonnet of the Landrover with his stick. "Up?"

"Up" he said again, giving the bonnet a whack with his stick.

I climbed up onto the bonnet and stood there looking around. A nice crowd was gathering.

"Now", he said, repeat after me, "Bleep Bleep I'm not a Jeep, I'm an 'effing Landrover".

Rather hesitantly I repeated it, "Bleep, Bleep, I'm not a Jeep, I'm an 'effing Landrover".

"Louder!" he shouted.

"Bleep, Bleep, I'm not a Jeep, I'm an 'effing Landrover".

"Louder!"

"Better" he said, "now turn around as you're saying it, that's it, keep turning around" he demanded. So there I stood, on the bonnet of the Sgt's Landrover, turning in circles and shouting, "Bleep, Bleep, I'm not a Jeep, I'm an 'effing Landrover".

"Keep going, " he called, "Until I get back" and off he went into the cookhouse to check the lunchtime meal.

Having suffered two humiliating incidents in one day, I vowed thereafter, to give the Sgt with the Red sash a very wide berth indeed.

As our final pass out parade grew closer, many of us, myself included, began to feel a little saddened that we were about to be split up. Of course, we would no doubt bump into one another during the course of our military careers, nevertheless, we hated to see 125 Training Party disappearing into the history books. I must admit that the last two or three rehearsals we carried out, in full No 2 Dress, and the Royal Engineer Band was most exhilarating.

There we marched, pounding our heels into the Parade Ground, so that we could be heard coming from half a mile away, chests out, arms shoulder high, heads back. It was grand. I could have marched up and down to the Royal Engineer Band until the cows come home.

Finally, the big day arrived, we were all tense and nervous, pacing up and down, taking extreme care not to scratch our bulled up highly polished best boots. These boots we had never yet worn. They had been lovingly worked upon most evenings and weekends for several months. To get a scratch on them now, before the Pass Off Parade would be a catastrophe of unprecedented proportions. Our Training Corporals gave us the once over, then a twice over, Sgt Steel turned up looking immaculate, and he gave us a once over. He looked more nervous than we did.

Peter, let me into a little secret, swearing me to keep hush-hush, he opened his suitcase from under his bed and took out a padded envelope. Making sure we could not be seen he opened it. Inside was a silver photograph frame containing the missing photographs of the twins. The frame was engraved 'In Appreciation', on the first line then, 'Room 1, 125 Training Party' beneath it. "So it was you who nicked it?" I accused. "Well, I couldn't very well ask him for it could I?" he responded.

There were loads of families and friends gathered on two stands either side of the parade ground. Between these, on the far side, was a smaller stand with a dozen or so Officers and their families. In front of this was the saluting dais. We heard Sgt Steel call us out on Parade, with heart pounding, and not without some emotion we all made our way out of the Spider. *The* Spider 10, which in just two or three hours, we must vacate and go our separate ways.

"You're family here?" Peter whispered.

"No, they couldn't afford the fairs", I whispered back.

248

"Welcome to join me, after the parade" he said.

"Thanks, Love to" I told him.

"Parade! Parade, Shun!" Shouted Sgt Steel.

"By the Right, Right Turn! By the Front, Quick March". There were three loud thumps from the base drum in Royal Engineer Band that had positioned its self in front of us. We were away. I could not possibly count the numerous parades I have taken part in all over the world during the next twenty-four plus years, they were always a thrill, but none, not one, ever came close to matching that band on that day.

As we marched around the square that day, from the corner of my eyes, I searched the crowds in the vain hope that someone, or Jamie, had managed to get down to the Pass Off parade. I searched in vain. Forty minutes later, having taken the Royal Salute, we marched past the Saluting Dais for the last time and to the tune of 'Wings' marched off the Parade Ground for the last time.

We were halted outside Spider 10. Inside were just empty lockers, bedsprings, and piles of suitcases, ready to be collected.

"To your duties" hollered Sgt Steel "Fall Out". Practically everyone turned to make there way back to the area of the Parade Ground where there was snacks and drinks made ready for our families and us.

"Room One," Peter called out, "As you were!"

The nineteen young lads from room one gathered around Peter. Peter handed Sgt Steel the padded envelope.

"Thanks Sarg" he said. "We couldn't have asked for a better Troop Sgt".

Sgt Steel coughed, slid out the silver photograph frame with the picture of his kids. He turned it around to read the brief inscription. A tear trickled and he wiped his cheek. I wiped mine too, and so did several others.

"You were the biggest load of time wasters and reprobates I have ever had the misfortune to have to try to turn into soldiers," he shouted at us. Wiping his other eye. "Now piss off the lot of yer" and with that he tucked his photo frame under his arm and walked back to his office. I met Sgt Steel some fifteen years later, as a Captain Quartermaster. He had that photo frame on his desk.

"Come on Ricky" said Peter giving me a nudge. We are missing the Party. Now totally unconcerned about our best boots, we ran back to the Parade Ground. As Peter and I approached the beer tent we saw a tall, well to do, looking Officer emerge, flat camp, tweed jacket with leather elbows, and wearing jodhpurs. Peter came to attention and saluted the old gent. "No need for that son", he said.

Peter turned to me "This is Ricky Houghton, remember, I told you about him"

"How could I possibly forget?" he said, putting out his hand and giving me a firm handshake.

"Met with old Miller!" Peter's father told me.

"Old Miller?" "Yes, Old Miller, you waited on for him the once!" he told me.

"Oh, that Old Miller?"

"Yes, said you are a proper card!" laughed the now Colonel Duncan-Forbes! He gave my shoulder a friendly punch!

"Poor old Provost Sgt eh!" he chuckled, and gave me a sly wink. "Come along old bean lets have a drink!"

Colonel Duncan-Forbes was a card himself and no slouch at putting away the beer either. Towards mid afternoon most families had disappeared, taking their offspring with them. There was a works party off to one side waiting patiently to start taking down the beer tent. The stands and Saluting Dais had long since gone. In the end it was Peter who insisted that the partying was over. He shook my hand, gave me a hug and a few pats on the back and said. "See you around, Ricky" he then took his Colonel daddy by the arm and led him off in the direction of his chauffer driven car.

I stood on the edge of the parade ground for a moment or two, turning full circle, taking in the cookhouse, the guardroom, the medical centre in the distance and Spider 10. The works party began dismantling the beer tents. I had reserves; I had a bottle stuffed into each of my trouser pockets. I took a leisurely stroll back to Spider 10.

When I walked in I took a last look at the Troop Notice Board. Everything that related to 125 Training Party had been removed. The door to the Troop Office was slightly ajar as usual.

"A week next Monday" Sgt Steel was telling someone "126 Training Party will form up in Transit Block,"

"Seems like a bloody conveyor belt doesn't it Sgt," One of the Cpls said.

"Yeah, I know" replied Sgt Steel, "But if they're 'alf as good as the last lot we'll be fine".

I scurried away, collected my suitcase, which still sat on the bedsprings of my old bed, and hurried out of the building.

Five minutes later, I was on the back of three ton truck, heading from Cove Railway Station. I never returned to Southwood Camp, Cove, and ten years later the whole place was demolished. Shame!

Chapter 21
UP, UP, AND AWAY!

When I left training I had been given one weeks embarkation leave and two weeks privilege leave, the privilege leave was deducted from my annual entitlement of twenty eight days, this included weekends! I would normally have flown to RAF Gutersloh at the end of the three weeks. I did not want to spend three weeks at my parents home. For one, I was worried about my health, for two, I couldn't afford to spend three weeks boozing it up every night and for three, I wanted to get to Germany as quickly as possible. Two weeks on leave in Germany would give me a chance to look around, get the feel of the place and perhaps get to know a few people before I had to report for duty. Of course I did not tell my family I could have stayed at home for three weeks. They would not be able to understand why I did not.

So there I was, twenty four hours after that magnificent Pass Out Parade, sitting in the Cross with Muth, Dad, Kev and Don. I had only drawn my three weeks pay, and had left any credits I had until I got to Germany. I was fairly well off, but I was being careful not to blow my whole three weeks pay in the five and a half days I had remaining at home. The family seemed to sense that and, believe it or not, we actually had one night in, in front of the television. We had watched Rawhide, Hancock's Half Hour and Panorama. With the exception of Kev all my family smoked.

I didn't realize just how much they had been smoking before I left home. With Muth & Dad puffing away on their Woodbines every five minutes or so and Don's Park Drive it was hard to watch TV through the smoke. "How come I never noticed before" I wondered.

Thursday Kev asked if I wanted to take part in a littler earner.

"What doing?" I asked.

"Oh, were helping a mate!" he said "He works for a firm that puts cigarette machines in pubs".

"What doing?" I asked again suspiciously.

"A lot of the mechanical machines are being replaced with electric ones, we are just helping remove the old machines, so that our mate can install the electric ones a bit later, speeds the whole process up".

"What you want me to do?" I asked.

"Oh just help cart the fag machines out to the van" he said, "tell you the truth, we could manage, but thought you might want a bit extra cash!"

"Where at?"

"Just around West Bromwich and this side of Birmingham".

"Nothing illegal?" Kev put his hands up in mock shock at such a suggestion.

"Illegal? Me? Never?"

"How much?" I queried.

"Oh! A Tenner, maybe fifteen quid" he replied nonchalantly.

"That much!" I exclaimed with surprise. "OK, count me in".

Kev took me out to his borrowed former bread delivery van, opened the back, and handed me a khaki cow gown. "Put that on" he ordered and jump in the back.

"Hmmm, still relegated to the back I see". I called out as Kev and Don jumped in the front.

"You might be a General" Kev called back "But just a General dogsbody to us" and they both broke out into hysterics.

About half an hour later, driving around West Bromwich, they had me lost in no time. We parked up the street from a pub. To my surprise Joseph White our big Jamaican friend came out. Gave Kev and Don a thumbs up sign and jumped into his own car. "Let's go," said Kev and we all piled out of the van. "That was Jo, wasn't it?" I asked my brothers,

"Who? Where, didn't see him, did you Don?" asked Kev.

"No!" said Don.

We entered the pub, "Wait here, whispered Kev. He approached the Bar.

"Hello Luv, Gaffer in?"

"Nah, out at the cash n carry I think" she replied.

"Got a hole in his head your Gaffa" moaned Kev, "Told him last week we would be here at eleven o'clock".

"Never said anything to me 'bout it luv" the buxom barmaid whined.

"Ok you two, I ain't paying you to hang around doing nothing, get it off the wall" Kev ordered.

"You're getting a new machine, you know, electric, with lights and everything".

"Oh are we?" asked the confused barmaid. Kev pulled his pen from behind his ear and wafts his clipboard under her nose.

Before she had time to focus her eyes, he pushed his pen under her nose, "just sign there me-duck." he told her with authority.

"What am I signing for?" she asked taking the pen. Kev waited until she had signed.

"It's just to show we are legitimate, we are not here to steal the bloody thing in broad daylight now are we?"

"I suppose not!" she replied thoughtfully.

While all this was going on at the bar, Don and me had unscrewed the cigarette machine from the wall and man handled it out to the van. I followed Don back into the pub. Gaffa usually lets us have a half" he informed the barmaid.

"Oh yes, sorry, silly of me, what will you have?"

"Three pints of your very best bitter luv" said Kev. As soon as the beers were served Kev told us "Don't take all day you idle buggers, we got work to do". We supped up quickly and left. We followed this Laurel and Hardy routine at six other public houses around the outskirts of town.

Funnily enough, we seemed to keep bumping into Joe White outside almost all of them. Twice he gave us a thumbs down. Gaffer is in so we moved on. At the end of a rather busy lunchtime, close to half past two, and close to closing time. Joe came up to the window. "Been to three pubs down this road. Words out Kev, We'll have to knock it on the head". "Oh well", says Kev "Got more than I had hoped".

He looked back at me in the back of the van hardly able to move with six cigarette machines crammed in with me, "Do us a favour Jo?" asked Kev, "Give Rick a lift back to our house".

"Sure thing!" replied Joe opening the back of the van and letting me out.

Back at home the cigarette machines were carefully emptied of all cash and cigarettes and split four ways. Except that I didn't smoke, so my share went to Muth and Dad. I also received some ten pounds, eleven shillings. I had never stolen anything in my life and I was unhappy and feeling very guilty about the afternoons events. I went as far as asking Kev and Don to, please, not get me involved in future. On the Sunday lunchtime, when the family and I went to the Cross for a farewell drink as per usual. I left the ten pounds, eleven shillings on the mantelpiece at home. I was sure Muth and Dad could make good use of it.

There had been no need for me to leave that Sunday lunchtime, I could have left much later that evening and still have had time to catch my afternoon flight from RAF Swindon but I was eager to be on my way. I wanted to be sure I would get to RAF Swindon in plenty of time. Having only travelled to Cove just the twice! I need not have worried; I arrived at RAF

Swindon a good seven and a half hours before my flight. The first six hours passed fine. I ate, drank, and read my JT Edson cowboy book. But now, with only an hour and a half to go I was pacing up and down, and even doing little jumps up and down with the sheer excitement of it.

"I, me, Ricky Houghton, from Friar Park, was going to fly". I had seen airplanes before of course, on the television, and as little silver specks crossing the sky ahead of a tail of white cloud.

When they finally called our group of passengers to the departure lounge I could barely contain myself any longer. I kept giving out little nervous giggles; I just could not help it. I was smiling that much the top of my head was in danger of falling backward. "I want a window seat, I want a window seat, I want a window seat," I kept telling myself, to remind me to tell the air hostess. "I wanted a window seat" when I walked up those steps and on to the aircraft. At last, I was next, "Identity Card Please Sir" asked the man, Sir? I looked behind me to make sure he wasn't talking to someone else. "Yes, You Sir," he said, "Identity Card Please". I took it out and thrust it under his nose. "Thank you, Sir" he said taking it from my hand and moving it away from his face so that he could focus his eyes on it. "That's fine, Sir" he said. I snatched the card and took the steps up into the aircraft two at a time.

At the top of the aircraft steps I gazed in awe, up and down the aircraft, "Welcome aboard" said this most beautiful of all angels. Tearing my eyes from her tight fitting white blouse with the faint outline of a white bra beneath I tried to avert my eyes; I looked up at the air vents. Breathlessly I asked. "Please may I have a window seat, miss". "You certainly can," she said guiding to a seat closest to the front, I sat near the window, "Your seat belt, Sir" she said.

"My what Miss?"

"Your seat belt" she said again, leaning right across my torso and fiddling down by my left hip. She pulled up one half of a seat belt. She fished for the second half and clipped them together across my lap. "There we are," she said, eyelids flashing ten to the dozen, "are you settled now?"

"Yes Miss".

I was waving my knees back and forth in sheer anticipation, leaning back and forward in my seat and rubbing my hands together endlessly. "I'm going to flyyyyyyyyy!". The announcements came.

"We shall be flying at a height of thirty thousand feet".

"Bloody hell" I told the steward checking our seatbelts, "Thirty Bloody Thousand Feet"

She smiled at me. I thought I'd died and gone to heaven.

"At a speed of six hundred and forty miles per hour!"

I jumped up and down in my seat, wriggling to free myself from the belt.

"Six hundred and forty miles land hour! Woweee!"

The next thing we were trundling along the runway and turning ready for take-off.

The engine noise increased. My sheer excitement increased along with it.

The engine roared. I roared along with it. I saw one of the stewards turn to look at me. She smiled again.

"Lift Off" I shouted as the wheels left the runway. I was so utterly delighted at being able to fly. I did not know anyone anywhere in Friar Park who had ever flown or would ever dream of flying. But I was.

Look out, Deutschland! Ricky Houghton is coming.

About the Author

I was born in Smethwick, West Midlands, England, above my grand fathers corner shop. My father, as did my grandfather before him, also served in the Royal Engineers. I did not see my father until I was six, going on seven and was raised in Whittington Barracks, Lichfield in Staffordshire. My father served two tours in Korea and also at Christmas Islands. When my father left the army in 1955, I went to live in West Bromwich in the heart of the Black Country. In the 1950s and early 1960s this part the country was Englands industrial heartland, the steel and motor industries in particular. As a result of the huge amount of air pollution in those years I suffered very badly with asthma and feared that my life long dream of following in my fathers footsteps would be denied me. However, with a little trickery, and the support of a close school chum, who sat my enlistment medical on my behalf, I did eventually succeed in enlisting. During the twenty four years that followed I served all over the world in a variety of capacities. I even, to the amazement of those who remember me as a child and as a scrawning seven stone teenager, succeeded in obtaining by sheer guts and determination the coveted Green Beret.

Printed in the United States
123648LV00001B/10/P

9 781434 398635